# CLOSE OF PLAY
# & PIG IN A POKE

A brilliant black comedy of manners, *Close of Play* is here republished in its definitive version following the première production at the National Theatre in 1979.

'What is impressive is the way Mr Gray combines his appreciation of mortality with social comedy and malevolent wit . . . He has skilfully combined his awareness of the confused mess we most of us make of our lives with a lively apprehension of the fact that in the end we are simply specks in the universe. To embody death convincingly on the stage is one of the hardest things for a dramatist to do: Mr Gray has here managed it in a way that, paradoxically, makes life itself that much more bearable.'

Michael Billington, *The Guardian*

Also included in this volume is a television play, *Pig in a Poke*, first transmitted in 1969 but published here for the first time. When Stephen and Wendy take possession of their trendy Hampstead home, they also inherit a slovenly sitting tenant in the basement. While Stephen chooses to immerse himself in the petty intrigues of the television play he's directing, Wendy's initial revulsion at the tenant's behaviour gradually turns to physical attraction . . .

*The photograph on the front cover shows Michael Redgrave in the National Theatre production of* Close of Play. *It is by John Haynes. The photograph of Simon Gray on the back cover is by Beryl Gray.*

Simon Gray

# CLOSE OF PLAY
# & PIG IN A POKE

EYRE METHUEN . LONDON

*Close of Play* first published in 1979 by Eyre Methuen
This volume, containing *Pig in a Poke* and a revised
version of *Close of Play,* first published in 1980 by
Eyre Methuen Ltd, 11 New Fetter Lane, London EC4P 4EE
Copyright © 1979, 1980 by Simon Gray
IBM set in 10 point Journal by 🔨 Tek-Art, Croydon, Surrey
Printed in Great Britain by Whitstable Litho Ltd,
Whitstable, Kent

ISBN 0 413 46960 3 (Paperback)

# CLOSE OF PLAY

**Close of Play** was first performed in the Lyttleton auditorium of the National Theatre, London, on 24 May 1979. The cast was as follows:

| | |
|---|---|
| JASPER | Sir Michael Redgrave |
| DAISY | Annie Leon |
| HENRY | Michael Gambon |
| MARIANNE | Anna Massey |
| BENEDICT | John Standing |
| MARGARET | Lynn Farleigh |
| JENNY | Zena Walker |
| MATTHEW | Adam Godley or Matthew Ryan |

*Directed by* Harold Pinter
*Designed by* Eileen Diss

**For Piers**

# Act One

*The Curtain rises on the stage in darkness. There is the sound of organ music, at first faint, then swelling until it fills the theatre. As it does so a faint pool of light spreads over* JASPER *in his armchair. He appears to be asleep. The music stops mid-chord.* JASPER *opens his eyes, as the rest of the lights come up steadily, until the room is filled with bright summer sunshine.*

*(Off, left, from beyond the french windows in the garden, the sound of children playing football.* HENRY's *voice sounds among theirs.)*

DAISY (*comes through on the run, goes to the french windows, calls out*). Henry — Henry dear — will you ask them to keep it right down — right down dear — because of the windows — oh, they can't hear — and as they're going to the Piece later on surely they can wait — and Marianne's forgotten Nindy's pottie again, can you believe. I know what she says about wee-wee being perfectly hygienic and Romans brushing their teeth in it but I don't like her putting her on our soup tureen, do you — but oh Good Heavens Jasper, you've got the lights on, didn't you realise dear, you don't need the lights now it's so light — it's not going to rain for a bit yet you know — (*turning them off*) — there — there, that's better isn't it, now then, tell me, what did you think of the dumplings, nobody's mentioned them, I was afraid they hadn't thawed right through and I saw your face when you bit into one, you didn't bite into ice, did you dear, I know how you hate cold in your mouth — it goes right through your system I know, is that what happened, did you bite on ice?

JENNY *enters, left, carrying a shopping bag.*

Oh there you are, dear, back already, that was quick.

JENNY. Is Matthew here?

DAISY. What, Matthew, no dear, isn't he with you? He ran after you to catch you up, didn't he Jasper?

JENNY. Oh, what a nuisance. Why on earth didn't he stay here, as I told him.

DAISY. What dear, well, never mind, you got the muffins did you, that's the main thing. (*Going to take them.*)

JENNY. Oh yes, well I'm afraid I could only get a dozen, Nanty, so I got half a dozen rock-cakes as well, I hope that's all right.

DAISY. What, what do you mean, but I ordered a dozen and a half muffins specially, didn't I Jasper? They promised to keep them, they swore they would, did you say who they were for, did you say they were for Professor Jasper Spencer?

JENNY. Well no, I think I said they were for you, Miss Blightforth —

DAISY. Oh well that explains it, you should have said Professor Jasper Spencer, they know his name in all the shops, don't they Jasper, particularly the baker's, well never mind dear, but rock-cakes you say, I don't know who's going to eat rock-cakes —

JENNY. Matthew loves them, I know.

DAISY. What, Matthew, well of course if Matthew — anyway how much is that I owe you, dear, the muffins are three and a half p. each I know, at least they were last week and they can't have gone up again in spite of the Common Market, can they Jasper?

JENNY. Oh please, let them be my contribution — as a matter of fact I —

DAISY. What, certainly not. Good Heavens, we wouldn't dream, would we, Jasper, you're our guests you know — so say three and a half p. the muffins, now Matthew's rock-cakes dear, how much were they?

JENNY. Oh four p. I think, but really Nanty —

DAISY. What, four p. Did you hear that, Jasper, four p. Matthew's rock-cakes! So that's three and a half times twelve equals forty-two, now, where's my handbag, the muffins plus six times four equals twenty-four, the rock-cakes, it was on the table, I know! Plus forty-two the muffins comes to sixty-six p. ah here it is sixty-six p. I owe altogether dear. (*Rooting around in her handbag.*) Oh but it's not here, but I'm sure I put it back after the milkman, Jasper do you know what I did with it?

JENNY. Actually Nanty, I do think I'd better get back to the High, you see Matthew's only got today off from school, I have to take him back first thing tomorrow. (*Moving off left.*) So I'll see you later.

DAISY. What, but it was here you know, you know the one Jasper, small, green, in velours, you gave it to me yourself, you know how careful I am —

MARGARET *enters through the arch.*

Oh hello dear, we're just looking for my purse, my small green one in velours, you haven't seen it have you?

MARGARET. No I'm sorry I haven't.

DAISY. That's strange, where on earth . . . thank you so much for the dishes.

MARGARET. The dishes?

DAISY. Helping Marianne with them, so sweet of you.

MARGARET. Actually Nanty, I'm afraid I didn't.

DAISY. What, oh then she's had to do them all by herself, oh dear, well — well never mind, she'll have finished them by now almost won't she Jasper, so you come and tell us all your news dear, it's so difficult at lunch isn't it, with all Henry's and Marianne's little ones, and it's such a long time since we've seen you and Benedict, we're dying to hear all about your adventures on that T.V. programme, we saw you, you know, did Jasper tell you, sitting there as cool as a cucumber with a beret on, wasn't it, and the way you talked to that little man with the working-class accent, where was he from, anyway?

MARGARET. Oxford.

DAISY. What, not the University, you don't mean?

MARGARET. Yes. All Souls —

DAISY. Good Heavens, Jasper, did you hear that, the little working-class man who interviewed Margaret was from Oxford, aren't you glad you didn't take that Chair after all, well you certainly put him in his place, dear, asking you all those questions and paying you those ridiculous compliments, and you just saying yes and no as if you couldn't be bothered with him to the manner born, I always say Jasper should have been on T.V., don't I Jasper, especially now they've got colour, because of his white mane you know, so distinguished, but I suppose they're not interested in Latin translations and mediaeval what-nots dear, you should have been a novelist like Margaret dear, and you could too, couldn't he Margaret, with his imagination, not that yours isn't very interesting too dear, oh yes I've read your novel you know, as soon as I heard you and Benedict were really coming down at last I went straight out and borrowed a copy from the library, didn't I Jasper?

BENEDICT *enters through the french windows.*

BENEDICT. Oh, you're in here, are you darling? I've been waiting for you in the garden for our little walk.

DAISY. Oh well, she's been talking to your father, dear, telling us all about her success and fame and what have you, you must be so proud of her, dear.

BENEDICT. What, Nanty?

DAISY. What, dear?

*There is a pause.*

Proud of her, I mean.

BENEDICT. Oh. Maggie you mean?

DAISY. Yes dear.

BENEDICT. Yes. Yes I am, Nanty. Very proud. (*Little pause.*) *Very* proud. Very very proud. Aren't I darling? Um — um — (*Sits down.*)

DAISY. Are you all right, dear? Is he all right?

BENEDICT. What Nanty?

DAISY. Are you all right, dear? You've been very quiet and grave, you know, all through lunch, and he hardly ate a thing Jasper, did he Margaret, you didn't touch the dumplings didn't you like them?

BENEDICT. Oh. Oh well I'm not very — very keen on food at the moment, am I darling?

DAISY. But you didn't speak either, hardly a word, and look at you now, not at all your usual self, is he Jasper — but I know — I know what you want to cheer you up, oh how silly of me to have forgotten when I went to all the trouble of remembering to get it in specially, but then it's your fault, it's been such a long time since you came to see us, now where did

I put it — oh in the hall — or — anyway Jasper you tell him all our news while I go and find it — I'll be right back dear. (*Going off left.*)

*There is a pause.*

MARGARET (*goes to* BENEDICT, *sits down beside him*). You're doing marvellously darling.

BENEDICT. What, darling?

MARGARET. Marvellously.

BENEDICT. I feel — I feel —

MARGARET. I can imagine, darling. I can.

BENEDICT (*emotionally*). I know. I know you can. Thank you darling. (*Looks towards* JASPER). Daddy — I — um — I know I owe you an explanation for not being in touch for such a long time. The truth is I've been going — going through rather a bad time, haven't I darling? And — and I didn't want to worry you. I expect you can guess what it was. My drinking. Well, not to put too fine a point on it, I wasn't just getting drunk now and then, which is what you must have thought, Daddy, I was actually on my way to becoming an alcoholic, wasn't I darling? So Maggie finally — bless her — put it to me that I had to choose. Between her and my scotch. And she meant it. Didn't you darling? She really meant it. So I — I put myself in the hands of a psychiatrist who had a very good reputation — at least some friends of Maggie's thought very highly of him, didn't they darling — Roger and Liza — but he turned out to be an old-fashioned, rather hard-line Freudian. So as far he was concerned, I was classic text-book stuff. Went into all my relationships — sibling rivalry of course — you know, that I'd always been jealous of Henry and Dick — Dick particularly, of course, said one of the reasons I drank was because I was guilty because I was glad that Dick was dead and — well, you can imagine — and you, of course, Daddy, which he got down to the old penis envy, naturally, and when I told him I'd never actually seen your penis so how could I envy it, it might be smaller than mine, after all — (*laughs*) well, that was in our first session, believe it or not — eventually he got on to Maggie, of course, said I envied *her* penis, didn't he darling, in the form of her talent, you see — and on top of all his — his clap-trap he was a pretty heavy drinker himself, I could smell alcohol on his breath and — well, by and large he was making things worse not better but of course the trouble was — I did develop a degree of dependence on him and — well, God knows what would have happened to me if I hadn't finally broken free — with the help of, well, Maggie of course, I can't tell you how wonderful — wonderful! she's been — but also of a new chap I happened to hear about at the B.B.C. — Vintross. Norman Vintross. It's because of him that I haven't touched a drop of scotch for what is it, darling, six, no, no, he insists on an absolutely ruthless accounting — it's part of his therapy, five, five weeks Daddy, isn't it darling?

MARGARET. Days, isn't it, darling?

BENEDICT. What?

MARGARET. Days, I think, darling.

BENEDICT. Yes, darling?

MARGARET. Didn't you say weeks.

BENEDICT. Oh, good God, did I really? (*Laughs.*) Days I meant of course, Daddy, six days. But when you think what I was up to — four bottles a day, Daddy.

MARGARET. More like three really, wasn't it darling?

BENEDICT. Oh now darling — well, between three and four — three and a half on a good day, bad day, that's what Vintross has to contend with, Daddy, so in my view he's a bit of a genius, quite simply. But absolutely practical, that's his great — his great, isn't it darling?

MARGARET. But he does fairly sophisticated things too, doesn't he darling, hypnosis for example.

BENEDICT. God yes, and you should see his eyes when he's putting me under, Daddy — brrr — like chips of blue ice, little chips of blue ice, aren't they darling?

MARGARET. Well, I've never met him, don't forget, darling.

BENEDICT. Oh. No, of course you haven't — but what he goes for above all is character, Daddy. In the traditional sense, rather like a Scots school-teacher, eh Maggie? Says I've only one basic problem. I'm weak. Feeble. Gutless. A moral no-hoper. So the only possible solution for types like me is to avoid drink altogether. To stay out of pubs and licensed restaurants — I virtually move with the luncheon voucher set now, Daddy, and he's even shown me a trick for dealing with

the B.B.C. parties I can't get out of — he says most of the
newsreaders have had to come to him at one time or another —
anyway, how to stand — look, legs splayed and hands locked
behind my back — (*does it*) to make it difficult to whip a
glass from a passing tray or otherwise receive one —

MARGARET. Darling, I think I'll go for a little walk.

BENEDICT. What, on your own, you mean?

MARGARET. Well, I think you and your father should have some
time together —

BENEDICT. Oh, well that's all right, isn't it Daddy? Don't go on
our account — unless you want to do a bit of creative mulling,
of course — did you know Maggie's just begun a new novel,
Daddy — last week — isn't that marvellous! and I expect she's
frightened that I'm going to launch into one of my panegyrics
about what she's meant to me — her support and — (*takes
her hand, kisses it*) and in fact you can thank her for our
getting down to see you at last, Daddy, she absolutely insisted
we come, didn't you darling — well then, don't be too long —
I'll miss you —

MARGARET *exits through door left.*

BENEDICT. Isn't she remarkable, Daddy? Oh, I don't just mean
in her talent, although that's remarkable enough God knows
when you think what the odds were against her finishing it. I
mean me, of course, I was the odds. Because you see Daddy —
oh, it sounds so bizarre now but in my worst phase — when I
was adding scotch to my breakfast coffee, you know *that*
stage, — I got it into my head that — well, that she was having
an affair. A real love affair, you see — and what made it more
dreadful, more nighmarish, was that I thought it was with
someone I knew but I didn't know who, if you follow — I knew
I knew the chap, even though there wasn't a chap at all — not
even evidence, Daddy, which of course simply made me more
insane. It got so I started to pick quarrels with friends, people
I work with at the Beeb, interpreting their remarks, their looks,
even — eventually even their smells — tried to sniff them, if
they'd been out of their offices a suspiciously long time — and
of course trying to catch poor Maggie in the act, taxi-ing home
at any hour, climbing in through the lavatory window so they
wouldn't hear me in the hall, then up the stairs in my socks,
flinging her study door open after crouching outside it for

hours — and there she'd be, typing calmly away, with her
glasses on, you know she wears glasses for her writing, and of
course the inevitable cigarette hanging from her lips, and she'd
give me such a distracted, absent-minded look, as if for a
second she didn't know who I was, let alone why I was there —
and so — more and more often I'd go well berserk — quite
berserk — and oh God — well the drink, you see, and knowing
she was being unfaithful and not knowing who with but
knowing I knew him and then realizing it was all a delusion —
but now when I think, think of the Hell I put her through,
what she's suffered — endured because of me — well even
Vintross, whose pretty tough about these things was appalled
when I told him — he said — he said that I — I — was a lucky
man to have such an unlucky wife — (*puts his hand to his eyes,
in tears.*) Sorry. Sorry Daddy — but I — I've always loved her
you know but now — now — sorry — I'll be — I'll be all right —
(*Sits, overcome.*)

DAISY (*enters from left, carrying a scotch bottle*). Upstairs — it
was upstairs in my bedroom, in the carrier bag, you see, the
one with the pink wool and the door-knob, anyway I've found
it, that's the thing — (*is pouring some into a glass*) I got it in
specially for you, because I remembered how you like to
settle down with a nice large one after lunch — there, dear, you
keep it beside you so you know where it is — what dear?

BENEDICT (*is staring appalled from the scotch to* DAISY).
Nothing. (*Laughs.*) Nothing Nanty that a — a Vintrossian gesture
(*Gets up.*)

DAISY. What, dear?

BENEDICT. I've just realised that I haven't — haven't given you a
proper cuddle yet Nanty — (*Goes over, puts his arms around her.*)
There, now I feel safe, eh Daddy? From temptation and harm.

DAISY. Aaaah — aaaah — I always say you're the feeling one, don't
I Jasper, feel things so quickly — anyway that's cheered you
up, has it, I knew it would, didn't I Jasper, and it's a malt, you
know — I asked for a malt — and now you can relax and tell us
some of your funny stories about your life at the B.B.C. — I
was just thinking the other day about my favourite, wasn't I,
Jasper, that Hugh Rhys-what's-it on the religious talks
programme of yours, the one who does the interviewing
sometimes, you used to keep us in stitches about, every time I
hear him talking things over with Bishops and atheists and such

I laugh out loud, I do, don't I Jasper, he sounds so solemn and Welsh but there he was getting himself locked in his office cupboard with his secretary and she thought — oh dear, all those scratches, poor man! (*Laughting.*) — And that quarrel with his wife over the dish-washer he insisted took saucepans and suds all over the kitchen floor short-whatnotting the fridge and the ice-cream gateau for his daughter's birthday melting into the fish for the cat — oh dear, oh dear — (*laughing*) what's he been up to recently, your Hugh Rhys-what's-it, something hilarious, do tell us?

BENEDICT (*who has moved away from* DAISY, *grinning fixedly, his hands locked behind his back*). He's — um — actually he's dead, Nanty.

DAISY. What dear?

BENEDICT. Dead.

DAISY. Good Heavens do you hear that, Jasper, Hugh Rhys-thing — but how, how dear?

BENEDICT. Oh it was a — well as a — what happened apparently — (*Stops.*)

DAISY. What dear?

BENEDICT (*looks yearningly towards the scotch*). Well — well actually Nanty do you mind — (*Goes and sits down some distance from the scotch.*) if we — I — I don't go into it at the moment I'm — you see it — it upsets me to think about it because in a way, well, in as much as I used to — to make him a bit of a butt and forgot how fond — how fond — you know what I mean, don't you Daddy, perhaps you could explain — explain to Nanty? (*Sits head lowered.*)

*There is a slight pause. Off, the sound of boys' voices, and* HENRY's *getting louder as they advance in a rush.*

*A ball bounces into the room and towards* JASPER.

DAISY. Of all the — of all the —

HENRY (*bounds in through the french windows breathing hard and sweating*). Oh golly — everyone all right?˙

DAISY. Well dear, it nearly bounced into your father's face, didn't it, Jasper?

HENRY. Oh, sorry Daddy — (*Takes the ball from* DAISY.) All

right boys (*going to the french windows*) now keep it down at the bottom — right to the bottom — (*Throws the ball out.*)

DAISY. Yes dear, but you see I can't help worrying about the windows —

HENRY. No, further down, Tom — right down — (*turns*) we're going to the Piece soon Nanty, so don't worry —

DAISY. I know dear, so couldn't they wait until then — because even at the bottom there are the outhouse windows —

HENRY (*has gone to the drinks table, squirted himself some soda water*). Whew! (*Draining it off.*) You were wise to stay out of that, Ben, I remind me of that chap, I told you about him, didn't I Daddy — (*Squirts some more.*)

DAISY. You do see what I mean, don't you dear?

HENRY. — did a dozen laps around the park in the sun, gulped down a jug of lemonade, dropped dead.

DAISY. I don't want to spoil their fun, you know that dear, but — what, Good Heavens, why?

HENRY. Bad heart, Nanty.

DAISY. Well then why did he do it, run a dozen times around in the heat, any fool knows that's madness, don't they Jasper, why did he dear?

HENRY. Well, actually, now I come to think of it, because I told him to, Nanty.

DAISY. What, oh well of course that's different dear — but why did you?

HENRY. I must have thought he needed the exercise, I suppose. Perhaps if he'd taken enough of it earlier, he wouldn't have killed himself taking it later.

DAISY. So really he only had himself to blame, you mean, dear.

HENRY. Well, no. Really he had me to blame, didn't he? Or would have, if he'd survived. But to be fair to myself I didn't tell him to do his running in the midday sun, nor to gulp down ice-cold lemonade afterwards. At least I hope I didn't. But on the other hand I certainly didn't warn him not to, either. But then I didn't know at the time he had a bad heart. And nor did he, come to that. Still, we got to the right diagnosis between us at the end, didn't we? Poor chap. I liked him rather a lot, he played the clarinet for the L.S.O., I always try not to think of him every time I hear that Mozart piece you're so fond of Daddy, how does it go — you remember it Ben? (*Tries to hum a few bars.*)

DAISY. Oh, I know — (*Hums it very pleasantly.*)

HENRY *joins in.* DAISY *and* HENRY *hum the opening section.*

HENRY (*squirts more soda water*). And here I am myself, my stomach packed with casserole, golly it was good Nanty, wasn't it Ben, *and* jacket potatoes and those doughy things —

DAISY. Dumplings, dear, did you like them?

HENRY. Oh damn!

DAISY. What dear?

HENRY. I'm on call today and I think I forgot to leave your number Daddy — well, I expect they'll know where I am. And anyway the call I don't make may save a life, eh? (*Laughs.*)

DAISY. Oh don't be silly Henry, you're a very good doctor, isn't he Jasper, isn't he Ben, a very good doctor, Henry —

MARIANNE (*enters from left flourishing a child's pottie*). Dum-dee-dee-dum-dum-dee-dee-dum — it was under my seat all the time, Nanty. In the van.

DAISY. What, oh good dear, I'm so glad — but isn't he a very good doctor, Henry?

MARIANNE. I should jolly well say he is, who says he isn't?

DAISY. Henry, dear.

MARIANNE. Oh ho, at it again, are we, hubby mine, I don't know what's been getting into him recently apart from the usual overwork, but the only thing wrong with him is that he's too jolly good a doctor, isn't he Gramps, and cares far too much and won't let himself let up for a minute, have you heard about his latest acquisition, I bet he hasn't even mentioned her, has he?

DAISY. Who, dear?

MARIANNE. Mrs O'Killiam, Nanty.

DAISY. Oh, is that the lady whose hair has been falling out, and wants a golden wig on the National Health —

MARIANNE. No no Nanty, that's poor old ga-ga Mrs MacDougall, no Mrs O'Killiam's a real case, in fact she's simply the most desperate case in the whole practice, Gramps, none of the others will touch her with a barge-pole.

HENRY. Now darling, that isn't quite true —

MARIANNE. Oh yes it is, darling, you know perfectly well her husband's in jail for some quite unspeakable offence against an eighty year old woman, Gramps —

DAISY. Why, what did he do to her?

MARIANNE. Well, for one thing he —

HENRY. Darling, I don't think — um you know —

MARIANNE. All right darling, for Nanty's sake —

DAISY. No no, I like hearing about things like that, don't I Japser?

MARIANNE. Anyway Gramps, as if that wasn't bad enough she's got two brutes of sons of about twelve and fourteen who are always in trouble with the police themselves —

HENRY. Well, of course with their background —

MARIANNE. Oh I know darling, absolutely *no* chance, and a little girl called Carla —

HENRY. Wanda, darling.

MARIANNE. Who's hydrocephalic, Gramps.

DAISY. What, dear?

MARIANNE. Water on the brain, Nanty. (*Holding her hands away from her head.*)

DAISY. Oh, we've got one of those, haven't we Jasper, he rides past here on his bicycle looking like Hmpty Dumpty poor thing —

MARIANNE. But the worst of it is she's in a hideous way herself, I shall never forget Henry's description of her the first time he saw her, Gramps, he said he said to himself as soon as he clapped eyes on her, 'Hello! Carcinoma!' didn't you darling?

DAISY. Hello who, dear?

HENRY. Although actually I was wrong, it's almost certainly a form of anorexia nervosa —

MARIANNE. Well, anyway, she's called him around every
    night this week, and after surgery too, he comes back looking
    grey with fatigue, Nanty — and this morning, Gramps, just as
    we were leaving one of her boys turned up and told Henry his
    mum wanted him straight away —

HENRY. But I really don't mind darling —

MARIANNE. Oh, I saw that look on your face before of course
    he said of course, Gramps, and you would have gone too,
    wouldn't you, if I hadn't asked him if it couldn't wait until
    this evening, and do you know what he said, you didn't hear,
    did you darling, the little squat one with the dribble and the
    funny lip, he said — well, he'd fucking well better come then.

DAISY. What dear?

MARIANNE. Sorry everybody, but that's what he said.

HENRY. Oh, it's his normal vocabulary, he talks to everybody
    like that, and I *am* on call darling.

MARIANNE. Yes darling, when aren't you on call? I'd better
    get this to Nindy before it's too late if it isn't already.

DAISY. Oh and thank you for doing the dishes, dear!

MARIANNE. What, oh golly, Nanty, did you mean for me to do
    them?

DAISY. What, you mean you haven't you mean!

MARIANNE. No Nanty, I'm sorry, I haven't.

DAISY. But I saw you at the sink, you see, so I assumed — I wish
    I'd known you weren't going to do them dear, because then I
    could have got them over and done with by now myself, you see.

MARIANNE. Well honestly Nanty, one moment we were all in
    the kitchen, and then Jenny'd gone —

DAISY. To get the muffins, dear.

MARIANNE. And then old Margaret had sloped off somewhere —
    and then you'd vanished —

DAISY. Only because I was worried about the ball and the
    windows —

MARIANNE. Oh golly, well let me deal with Nindy and I'll come
    back and do your dishes for you, all right? (*Goes out through
    the french windows.*)

DAISY. No no dear, I'll do them, I don't mind doing them, oh I do hope she didn't think I meant, Henry you don't think she thought I meant —

HENRY. No no Nanty, of course she didn't — but hey, I haven't asked after your headaches — Nanty's been getting some very bad headaches, Ben, hasn't she Daddy — (*Putting his arm around* DAISY.)

DAISY. Oh they've been terrible recently, haven't they Jasper? I've tried doing what you said, lying on a hard surface in a dark room with moist pads over my eyes, but it doesn't stop the throbbing or the nose-bleeds, does it Jasper?

HENRY. Nose-bleeds?

DAISY. Oh yes, terrible nose-bleeds and a humming in my ears and seeing things double —

HENRY. I see. Well, Nanty, I think we ought to have someone take a proper look at you. I can't promise he'll cure them but I won't let him make them any worse.

DAISY. Oh Henry — aaah — so kind, so thoughtful — oh and look dear, tell Marianne she's not to touch the dishes, I never meant her to, you know — they won't take a minute tell her — (*Going out through the arch.*)

HENRY. Actually Daddy, I think I'd better try and fix up an appointment for Nanty as soon as possible — nothing to worry about, just a few tests, X-rays, that sort of thing — all quite routine, but to put our minds at rest, we don't want anything happening to our Nanty, do we, Ben?

BENEDICT (*who has been gazing at floor, hands locked*). Mmmm?

HENRY. You all right?

BENEDICT. Oh. Oh well um — yes, yes. Thanks.

HENRY. I must say it's terrific to have you here again after all this time.

BENEDICT. Oh. Yes. Thanks. Thanks Henry.

HENRY. And Maggie too.

BENEDICT. Oh she was very keen to come. Very keen. Very very keen.

HENRY. Oh. Well that's flattering, eh Daddy? Where is she, by the way, I've hardly had a chance to speak to her.

BENEDICT. No.

HENRY. What?

BENEDICT. What?

HENRY. Maggie?

BENEDICT. Oh. Oh yes.

HENRY. Has she gone out?

BENEDICT. Yes. Yes I think so, yes. For a walk, hasn't she Daddy — something to do with her novel you see. She gets these fits. Inspiration, I suppose. Yes.

HENRY. Are you sure you're all right, Ben?

BENEDICT. No. No I seem — something slightly wrong with my — my stomach — perhaps those doughnuts in the casserole — but very queasy.

HENRY. I'll get you some Alka Selzer, where is it Daddy?

BENEDICT. What — oh no, no, not Alka Selzer, never works for me besides I don't want to make a fuss — I'll tell you — I'll tell you what, (*getting up*) perhaps a drop — just a little drop of this might do something for me (*picks up the glass with a trembling hand, takes an enormous gulp*) have to be careful though, eh Daddy, no back-sliding, eh, you see, Henry, I was telling Daddy, I've given this stuff up virtually at last, haven't I, Daddy? I go to a chap, you see.

HENRY. A chap?

BENEDICT. Yes. His name's Vintross. A bit of a genius in my view. He's been treating me for — things.

HENRY. Oh. A psychiatrist.

BENEDICT. No. A pediatrician, actually. But he does things like me on the side. Privately. God you should see his eyes when he's doing hypnosis, I was telling Daddy about them, wasn't I, Daddy? (*Pouring himself more scotch.*) They're the deepest brown eyes I've ever seen, and they burn, burn, down — he's bloody expensive, you can imagine.

HENRY. Yes. Yes. I can.

BENEDICT. But then that's part of his treatment, you see. Charges the equivalent of a double scotch for every three minutes of his time, he worked it out at. You're not cured, he said, until you get my bill. If you can look at it without taking a drink, there's hope, and if you pay it you won't be able to afford a drink, apart from meths, of course, and if you don't pay it, I sue. (*Laughs.*) Vintage Vintross, that is. Jokes are a part of his style.

HENRY. Oh — oh well he sounds just the job, doesn't he Daddy?

MATTHEW *enters through left door, stands uncertainly.*

Oh hello Mat, and what have you been up to?

MATTHEW. Oh — um — well um — nothing um — (*Laughs.*)

HENRY. How's the soccer coming?

MATTHEW. Oh — well I mean um — you know.

HENRY. Made a team yet?

MATTHEW. Well — just the house team.

HENRY. Oh, well that's jolly good — isn't it Ben — congratters, Mat.

MATTHEW. Oh — well, um, thanks. (*Laughs.*)

HENRY. Oh and hey, I don't know if Marianne mentioned to you — we're taking the boys to the Piece soon for a footer around — why don't you come along and show them what you can do, and then show me how to do it, eh?

MATTHEW. Oh — well — I — Mummy asked me to go for a walk with her, you see — I — I — was meant to meet her at the baker's but well, you haven't seen her?

HENRY. She hasn't been through here.

MATTHEW. Oh well, she's probably gone looking for — I'd better — better go and see if — um — (*Makes towards the exit, left.*)

HENRY. Anyway we'll be on the Piece later if you *do* want a game —

MATTHEW. Right — right — (*He goes out.*)

BENEDICT (*who has poured himself more scotch*). God he's getting like Dick isn't he — it makes the brain to reel and the heart to lurch how like Dick he's getting, doesn't it, is he top-dog at school, the way Dick used to be?

HENRY. Well actually that reminds me — I was going to mention it Daddy — and I'm glad you're here Ben, you can tell me what you think — you see I had a letter from his housemaster the other day, he seems to think of me as in sort of loco parentis and he didn't want to worry Jenny with it — but he's a little concerned about our Mat. Says he's been rather withdrawn this term — well, since Dick's death — well, I suppose that's hardly surprising, but apparently although he's dropped every one of his old chums he's taken up with a boy — well, quite a bit younger than himself and — in a nutshell, the housemaster isn't too keen on it. Thinks it's all a bit too hot-housey. That's why he's wangled Mat into the football team, to make him mix more you see, although actually Mat's not too good at football, but then this friend of his doesn't play at all. He's an asthmatic.

BENEDICT. Ah-hah! One of those, eh?

HENRY. What? Well, you see what troubles me is I'm not sure he should interfere at all — I mean, the football's all right, *if* Mat comes to enjoy it — but otherwise well this relationship may be filling an important need, mayn't it, and then given how delicate — delicate these matters are, especially at that age — well, what do you think, Daddy?

BENEDICT (*laughs*). God, doesn't it bring it back though?

HENRY. What?

BENEDICT. All of it — the sodomy, buggery, public-school duggery — much more fun than State schools. In State schools you give them ten quid a week, kit them up with contraceptives, hand them a list of V.D. clinics, pack pot into their lunch-boxes, nothing furtive, nothing passionate, nothing to prepare them for life — hey, remember old Prothero, Hen, old Prothero, did we ever tell you about old Prothero, Daddy, used to come and sit on the edge of the bed after lights, tucking in the middle-school chappies, and if there'd been a caning he'd want to inspect the stripes, put on ointment —

HENRY. Golly yes, old Cheeks! (*Laughs.*)

BENEDICT. That's it! Cheeks — Cheeks Prothero! Had a crush on Dick, didn't he Hen — and old Coote — Coote Wilson — and — all of them come to think of it, didn't they Hen? Had crushes on Dick, fighting over him they were! Like bloody monkeys! God, I'm glad you sent us to one of the best schools in the country, Daddy, aren't you Hen?

HENRY. I certainly don't think it did us any harm.

BENEDICT (*pouring himself another drink*). Vintross is queer. Gay, I mean. Did I tell you?

HENRY. Is he? No, you didn't.

BENEDICT. He's got this Filipino house-boy. Opens the door, takes your coat. Got a pretty beaten look to him, so I expect there's a cupboard full of things, eh, handcuffs, leg-irons, whips, masks, S.S. uniforms, that sort of gay, you see. Ballsy-gay. Sometimes his eyes go just like a cat's — a vicious green. You know?

HENRY. The house-boy's?

BENEDICT. Vintross's. Vintross's eyes.

HENRY. I thought you said they were brown —

BENEDICT. No, no. Green, eh Daddy? Vicious green. Like a cat's.

HENRY. How's the stomach?

BENEDICT. Flat as a board. Keeps himself in top nick, you see. Probably with the Filipino, eh? (*Laughs.*)

HENRY. No, I meant yours. Is it settling down?

BENEDICT. Oh. Well still a bit — hey Hen I must show Hen, eh Daddy — Vintross's party posture — look — hands so — feet thus — (*tries to adopt it, still holding his glass, stumbles backwards*). Oooooooops!

HENRY *catches him.*

Thanks. See what I mean, bloody difficult.

HENRY. Yes. (*Watches him, looks anxiously towards* JASPER.) Oh — that reminds me — that little Welsh friend of yours, the one that got his finger stuck in his flies at the Israeli Embassy — we were having a good laugh about him just the other week, weren't we Daddy? What's he been — ? (*Laughing.*)

BENEDICT (*laughing*). Old Hugh Rhys — um —

HENRY. Yes —

BENEDICT (*stops laughing*). Oh. Dead, Henry.

HENRY. What?

BENEDICT. Dead. Yes. Dead.

HENRY. That little Welsh — good God, good God, but — but well how, Ben, what happened?

BENEDICT. Killed himself. Didn't he Daddy? Telling Daddy and Nanty earlier —

HENRY. But why?

BENEDICT. Don't know Henry. Don't know. All I know is that one night last week he got out of bed, told his wife he wanted some air, walked up to Hampstead Heath, took off his trousers, hanged himself.

HENRY. With his own trousers?

BENEDICT. They found a washing-line too, but it had got tangled in the tree.

HENRY. And he didn't leave a note — nothing to explain —

BENEDICT. Oh yes. He left a note. Pages and pages in fact. Must have spent the day writing it — alone in his office — pages and pages — pinned them to his shirt.

HENRY. Well, what did it say?

BENEDICT. Don't know. It rained during the night. Illegible. Every word. Pathetic, eh Daddy? Poor little Hugh Rhys — um —

*There is a pause.* HENRY *releases a sudden wild laugh.*

BENEDICT. What?

HENRY. Oh I'm sorry — so sorry — don't know where that came from — I certainly didn't mean any disrespect to Hugh — Hugh Rhys um —

BENEDICT. That's all right, Hen, we know why you laughed, don't we Daddy, matter of fact I laughed myself when I heard — I mean trousers, tangled washing-line, unreadable suicide note — like all the other stories I used to tell about him. Right?

HENRY. Well yes, I suppose —

BENEDICT. Except this time he's dead, of course. That's the difference. But a big one. Crucial, in fact.

HENRY. Yes. Yes indeed.

BENEDICT. Isn't that right, Daddy? (*Pours himself more scotch.*) And of course appropriate. Hugh Rhys — um's death. An appropriate death. Like Dick's, in a sense. Eh? (*There is a pause.*) I mean, you think of Dick, the brightest and the best of us, eh, we know that, Daddy, don't we Henry, well of course he was, because he was just like you, Daddy, wasn't he, fellowships just like you, lectureships just like you, a readership just like you, would have ended up with a professorship just like you. Maybe even an O.B.E., Daddy, just like you, and then a wife he loved, just like you, Daddy, I mean you loved Mummy didn't you, the tragedy of your life her death, wasn't it, if you see, and a son he adored, just as you adored him, and is turning out just like him as he went on turning out just like you. Apart from being dead. Just like Mummy. See Daddy.

HENRY. No. No. I don't think we do see, quite, Ben. But perhaps we shouldn't discuss —

BENEDICT. No no, look at it this way. Where was Dick different from Daddy? Where? A bit raffish, right? Bit of an adventurer, right? (*Laughs.*) Reckless. Reckless and raffish — not like Daddy, eh, nobody's ever called you reckless and raffish, have they, Daddy? And so his motor-bike. See. See how it fits?

HENRY *looks towards* JASPER.

BENEDICT. Roars over here, has one of his intimate chats with Daddy, and then later, far too late, when he was tired, his head spinning with Daddy's ideas and jokes and anecdotes and gossip, eh Daddy? What does he do? Does he stay the night? Upstairs in bed in his old room? Does he stay the night? No. Not old Dick. Back, back on his motor-bike, roaring off again — past Newmarket, past Baldock, Royston, Hitchin — faster and faster, and then off — off the road — hurtling right off the road and over the bank and into the tree into the dark! And we say — *we* say — if it hadn't been for his motor-bike Dick'd still be alive. True. But — but if it hadn't been for Daddy, then he wouldn't be dead. Vintross says. (*Pours himself more scotch.*) Now do you see?

HENRY. Well — um, Ben — look, what would Vintross say if he could see the amount of scotch you're knocking back, old chap?

BENEDICT. Say it was quite all right. As long as I can cope with it in a situation I can't cope with without it. That's what he'd say.

JENNY (*enters left*). Oh sorry — but has he come back, Matthew?

HENRY. Yes. But he went out again — I think he was looking for you —

BENEDICT. Hey Jen, we were just saying about Matthew — so like Dick, isn't he? So like him?

JENNY. Yes — yes I suppose he is —

BENEDICT. Henry was telling us about that letter he got from his housemaster — on his little sexual problems — don't you pay any attention, Jen, Dick had the same, used to steal too, didn't he, Hen, has Matthew started stealing yet? Well, don't worry, if he turns out like Dick he'll be all right, eh? Apart from being dead, I mean.

JENNY. Matthew's housemaster wrote to you?

HENRY. Yes, well it was just a — nothing to — didn't want to bother you —

JENNY. I see. Which way did he go, Matthew?

HENRY. Out the front way I think — but Jenny really —

JENNY *goes out left.*

HENRY. Golly Ben, I do wish you hadn't mentioned that to Jenny.

BENEDICT. What? (*Pouring himself more scotch.*)

HENRY. About Matthew. I did say it was confidential, didn't I, Daddy?

BENEDICT. Oh. Right. But there's another thing. The funeral. We've never talked about the funeral, have we, remember it, Daddy? Our standing there in the Chapel and they brought him in and put him down on that conveyor belt and that lady started on her organ, that old lady with the deaf-aid. And then the door in the wall, the trapdoor in the wall slid open, and he began to slide towards it and then through it, remember Hen? You don't do you?

HENRY. Of course I do, it's just that — well I don't think we should —

BENEDICT. Well, what happened? What happened as he slid through?

*There is a pause.*

You don't want to say, do you? Well, I don't mind saying. I'll say it, Daddy. What happened as he slid through is — I threw up. That's what happened. Isn't it? Because I was drunk. (*Pause.*) You know, I used to be pretty ashamed about that. Thought I'd disgraced the whole proceedings. That's what I thought. (*Drinks.*) Until Vintross put me right. Know what he said, Vintross? He said it doesn't matter whether you're drunk or sober, sober or drunk, the coffin slides through just the same, the door in the wall slides open just the same, same old lady plays an organ just the same — and then, next please! Next please! You can't disgrace it because you can't even interrupt it. Unless there's a resurrection of course! (*Laughs.*) Just a business, disposing of the dead. That's how he cuts through things, old Vintross. Right to the heart. (*Pours himself more scotch.*)

HENRY (*goes to him*). Ben that's enough. Quite enough. (*Tries to take the bottle away.*) Think of Daddy —

BENEDICT. What?

HENRY. Think of Daddy! (*Low and intense.*)

BENEDICT. Think of — oh oh shit-eating time come round again, eh Henry. Shit-eating time. Well let me tell you something else Vintross says.

HENRY. I don't think we want to hear anything else Vintross —

BENEDICT. He says — he says the trouble with me — he says the reason I was nearly an alcoholic virtually until he got his hands on me — was that all my life I've been made to eat shit, I've been the family shit-eater — apologise, explain, grovel — and he said — when I told him Maggie wanted me to come up he said — go — he said go — but on no account — never — never — again — for any reason — was I to eat shit. Never again, not for you, not for Daddy even. No more shit-eating. See! Never!

*There is a pause.*

MARIANNE (*enters through the french windows laughing*). Darling I must show you — (*Shows Henry contents of pot.*)

HENRY. Golly, yes!

MARIANNE. It was Gramps' magic, honestly Gramps! She sat there straining and straining until I said do it for Gramps! And out it came. Gushing!

HENRY. Golly!

MARIANNE. What she must have gone through holding it back, poor darling — anyway, thank you Gramps — and darling, they really are a bit desperate about going to the Piece, they're loading themselves into the van, so if you'd just give this a sluice — (*Hands HENRY the pot.*)

*There is a long honk from off, left.*

Oh oh — I told Tom not to — anway I'll see you out there —
(*Sees* BENEDICT.) Is everything all right?

HENRY. Oh yes, fine, fine, just having a jaw!

MARIANNE. The three chaps together, eh, jolly good for Gramps.
(*Goes out left to another long honk*.)

*There is a pause.* HENRY *looks at* BENEDICT, *looks at* JASPER,
*looks at* BENEDICT *again, puts down the pot, goes over. Puts a
hand on* BENEDICT's *shoulder.*

HENRY. We never knew you felt like that, did we, Daddy? But
Ben I promise you I've never wanted you to eat — and nor has
Daddy, I know — but perhaps it was important for you to say it,
eh Daddy, and get it out of your system once and for all.

BENEDICT. Old Hen. (*Puts a hand on* HENRY's *hand on his
shoulder*.)

HENRY. Old Ben.

BENEDICT. Old Hen.

HENRY. You don't think you ought to lie down now? You look
— um —

BENEDICT. No — no — I'm all right now. Purged, you see.
Purged. Just as Vintross said.

HENRY. Well that's — that's —

*Low honk, off.*

HENRY. Oh I'd better — (*Looks towards* JASPER, *smiles
reassuringly*.) You um — well, you won't have any more of that
though, will you?

BENEDICT. What? Oh no — no — don't need it now — just want
a nice calm chat with Daddy now. That's all. Eh Daddy?
Talk over old times. Without — without any — eh Daddy?

HENRY. Good. That's the job, eh Daddy? Well then, see you both
later. (*Goes out left.*)

BENEDICT. God, I love Henry, don't you, Daddy? Oh I know
Dick was always his favourite brother and he was always Dick's
favourite brother and I was the one left out from their
favouritism, but God how I loved them both. I suppose that's
what I was, am, Daddy, when you think about it a — a sort of
only son with two favourite brothers and a dead mother and a
— a father who — who — well, why should you? Nobody has to.

*(Gets up, pours himself more scotch.)* Nobody. Vintross says —
*(Gulps down scotch.)* My Maggie's frightened of the dark. Did
you know that? My Maggie? I hold her against it very tight,
tight against it, and I say don't be afraid Maggie, don't be
afraid my Maggie, I'm here — Ben's here, Ben's here — and
when I painted her study up for her I did it in light colours,
pastel colours Daddy, and I bought her a typewriter, and I
change her ribbons you know, all she has to do is the writing
you see, clackety-clackety, clackety-clackety —
pages on pages, chapters on chapters, clackety-clackety-
clackety, and then when I come back, grey with fatigue, back
from the B.B.C., and loving her and holding her and changing
her ribbons — up I go to see her, longing to see her — and looks
at me — she looks at me as if I wasn't there, Daddy, and never
had been. Never had been. But *he'd* been all right, *he'd* been —
I catch the whiff of him now and then, smell the smell of his
spoor on her, smell it all over her, on my Maggie, and I know
who it is, I know who it is, and one day I'll get him by his
whiff, the whiff of his spoor, or catch them at it, the two of
them. Whoever he is. At their fuckity-fuckity, clackity-fuckity,
fuckity-clackity! *(Lurches sideways.)*

DAISY *(enters through the arch).* What dear? Having a nice chat
the two of you that's nice dears, I've done the dishes, just as
well as Marianne's gone off to the Piece, I heard the honking, I
do wish he wouldn't, Jasper, it's little Tom you know, sets my
head off, and now the mat — the mat's gone from the back-
kitchen, would you believe Jasper, after I put it down specially,
so I've got to get the one from the front — and how are you
feeling now, dear, you look much more relaxed, doesn't he
Jasper, much more yourself dear, that's good — *(Goes out left.)*

BENEDICT. What? *(Stumbles after her. Stops.)* And do you know
what Vintross says about her, Daddy, says she made me eat
shit too, when I was little, because she wanted to be our
Mummy, and when she couldn't be our Mummy made me eat
shit to make up —

DAISY *(returns carrying a large doormat).* For the mud you see.

BENEDICT. — when I was little —

DAISY. What dear?

BENEDICT. Saying Vintross says — Vintross —

DAISY. Who dear? Oh, that little Welsh friend of yours, so sad, so sad —

BENEDICT. When I was little, Nanty, you made me eat and eat and eat.

DAISY. What, oh well dear, I did my best to keep your tummy full, of course I did, didn't I Jasper, but then you were such a greedy mite, you know, wasn't he Jasper, like Oliver Twist dear, always asking for more. (*Laughs.*)

BENEDICT. Wanted to be our Mummy, didn't you Nanty? Take the place of my Mummy?

DAISY. What — oh oh — oh no — I knew I could never take *her* place, didn't I Jasper, even though people said we were almost look-alikes — didn't they, Jasper — not usual you know in second cousins once removed except she had golden hair that came right down her back to sit on, sit on her own hair, she could, couldn't she Jasper, oh really very glamorous your mother dear, aaaah, such a pity she didn't live to see what you've become! — Isn't it, Jasper?

BENEDICT. What?

DAISY. She adored you all, didn't she Jasper?

BENEDICT. Me? Adored me? Me too?

DAISY. Well dear, it was different with you, you were just an insigificant scrap at the time, and always crying for a feed, you know, while Henry was bigger and she could talk to him and Dick — well Dick, she idolised, Dick — but then we all did, didn't we Jasper? Because he was so pretty and clever.

BENEDICT *laughs.*

What dear?

BENEDICT. Dead, Nanty. Gone. Pretty Dick. Clever Dick. Through the door in the wall. On his motor-bike.

DAISY. Yes, dear, I know dear. So sad.

BENEDICT. Why didn't you stop him?

DAISY. What dear?

BENEDICT. Why didn't you stop him, Nanty. Killing himself. Why?

DAISY. Oh really Benedict, oh really dear, I've told you before, haven't I Jasper, every time you come down dear I've told you, you can't have forgotten, can he Jasper, I've told you and told you dear I told him not to, didn't I Jasper, and if he'd listened to me it wouldn't have happened, would it Jasper, it's late I said, you're tired I said, stay the night, make him stay the night, Jasper, didn't I Jasper, and he said, what was it he said, or was it you Jasper, one of you said, oh nobody can stay the night Daisy or Nanty whichever of you it was said it, and they both laughed, the pair of them, and off he roared, off he roared, poor silly boy, in that helmet pulled down and those great gauntlets, and his head so low over the handle-bars, roaring off, and I knew, I knew, if he'd listened to me it wouldn't have happened, would it Jasper, but then nobody listens to me, it was just the same with your mother you know, when I told her to go straight to the doctor with that lump, I knew that lump as soon as I saw it, didn't I Jasper, Rose, I said, Rose, Rose —

BENEDICT *stumbles towards the door, left.*

What, where are you going, dear?

BENEDICT (*in a child's voice*). Old room, Nanty, lie down in my old room when I was little Nanty —

DAISY. There's a good boy, aaaah, but oh, not your old room dear, Matthew's in there, and all his things and Jenny's using Dick's of course, they're staying the night you see, so you use Henry's dear — Henry's old room —

BENEDICT *goes out.*

(*As she speaks the stage begins to darken.*) Did he hear, oh I hope he heard, he always makes such a mess when he comes down, not that it isn't lovely to see him, for your sake. I know dear, but sometimes I think he tipples (*lifts her hand to her mouth in a drinking movement*) a little too much, it's all very well to say he needs relaxing but not when he turns things upside down, and he takes after Rose that way, she liked her glass too, but of course she didn't let it go to her head like that, and oh why did he have to upset me with remembering Rose and Dick poor dears, and now my head, pounding because of the honking, pounding you know — and all the times I've asked them not to let Tom — but then it's true, true nobody listens to me, they go in and out and don't do the dishes and make fusses but not one of them says about tea, what am I meant to do about tea, Jasper, do I lay for everybody on the assumption or what, do I, do I lay on the assumption, that's what I want to know Jasper, well, that's what comes of letting them treat me as housekeeper, that's what they think I am, well it won't do, it's not good enough, it's time they were told what I really am, and you should tell them dear, yes, it's up to you to tell them, Jasper, now we've got them all together and — oh, good Heavens, oh no (*seeing the pot*) what's this doing — but it's half full, you see, you see what I mean — left for me to — sometimes I think Marianne — no wonder my head — my poor head — (*begins to go out under the arch*) and oh, the windows, I'm locking the windows so they can't come in this way (*shuts them*) and tramping mud (*locks them*) there, there, at least I won't have mud this time — (*Going out through arch.*)

*The stage continues to darken to half-light.*

JASPER *lets out a sudden, terrible groan. Puts his head back.*

*Curtain.*

# Act Two

*The same. About an hour later.* JASPER *as before. The stage is in semi-darkness. It is raining heavily. There is a sudden rattling at the windows.* MARIANNE's *voice,* HENRY's *urgently, with the cries of children.*

MARIANNE (*off*). Gramps — Gramps —

HENRY (*off*). Daddy — Daddy — can you hear me!

DAISY (*enters on the run through the arch*). No, no, not there — not that way — oh it's so dark — (*turns on the lights*) I've opened the back-kitchen door — I've put a mat down in the back-kitchen — the back-kitchen dears please —

HENRY. For Heaven's sakes Nanty, we're getting — all right, but you go in that way, darling. I'm not having you get any wetter — Nanty — Nanty — open the door for Marianne!

DAISY. What, oh — (*opens the french windows*) oh, there you are dear, are you all right? I didn't mean you of course, just the children — I wanted to make sure they'd go around by the back-kitchen where I've put another mat especially you see —

MARIANNE (*during this enters, with a man's raincoat over her head, in Wellington boots*). I must say Nanty, I didn't expect you'd actually lock the door on us — but golly, what a business — (*Taking off her raincoat.*)'

DAISY. Here dear — let me — (*Taking the coat.*)

MARIANNE. One minute thumping the ball about, the next absolute buckets, like the Old Testament, Gramps — (*Lifts a leg.*) I say Nanty, do you mind —

DAISY. What, oh. (*Pulls at the boot.*) And the one in the back-kitchen had gone, I think the boys must have — (*Pulls the boot off.*)

MARIANNE (*staggering back*). Whhoops!

DAISY. All right dear? You know for football posts, I know they do sometimes.

MARIANNE *lifts the other leg.*

DAISY (*pulls if off*). So I had to put the one from the front door down — there, there we are —

MARIANNE. Thank goodness we had our bad weather gear in the van — we had to sprint like billy-oh to get it and then we thought Nindy had dropped her pot —

DAISY. What, oh no dear, her pot was here, where you left it. Half full and more.

MARIANNE (*laughing*). Yes, Henry remembered after we'd sent poor old Nigel haring back for it with my plastic bonnet over his head —

DAISY. I suppose I'd better go and put these —

HENRY (*enters under the arch, towelling his head*). Phew, what a soaking —

DAISY. Oh Henry, you saw the mat, did you?

HENRY. What, Nanty?

DAISY. The mat. I put down the mat.

HENRY. Oh.

DAISY. Well, they did use it, dear, didn't they, I had to get it round from the front, you know, because the one at the back — I think the boys — must have taken it for their football —

MARIANNE. No, they didn't Nanty. They haven't touched it, not after all the business last time when they were using it as a sleigh and you were jolly sharp with them.

DAISY. Oh, well as long as they've used the one I've just put down, they did didn't they, Henry?

HENRY. Well, actually Nanty, there wasn't a mat there.

DAISY. What, what do you mean. I've only just put it there, haven't I, Jasper? It can't have gone too.

HENRY. Well, Nanty, I can assure you, there's no mat there.

DAISY. Where?

HENRY. The kitchen.

DAISY. The kitchen! But I told you to go by the back-kitchen — I opened the back-kitchen door especially — I told you —

HENRY. Oh sorry, I just heard kitchen —

DAISY. Oh good Heavens — and after all the trouble I went to — well where are they now, what are they doing, and there'll be mud on their boots — where are they?

HENRY. Now now, Nanty, don't panic, I've told them to take off their shoes and dry and wash themselves and to sit quietly down at the table.

DAISY. The table, which table?

HENRY. Well, the kitchen table.

DAISY. Why?

HENRY. Well, for their tea.

DAISY. Their tea! But they can't have digested their lunches yet!

MARIANNE. Well, you know the boys, they can be digesting their lunches while they're eating their tea — (laughs.)

DAISY. But I've laid for everybody, haven't I Jasper, I've laid for everybody, a proper family tea — muffins and — rock-cakes even —

MARIANNE. Oh, they don't need muffins and rock-cakes, just some bread and butter and marmite and milk —

HENRY. We'll do it, Nanty, no need for you to bother yourself.

DAISY. Oh, it's not bothering myself I mind, I'm used to that, aren't I, Jasper, the point is I laid tea for everybody, as nobody told me any differently, can't they wait?

HENRY. They can't really, Nanty, no. I know it's unreasonable of them, to be at the age when they're permanently hungry —

MARIANNE. And anyway Nanty, as you won't allow them anywhere *but* the kitchen — and what can they do there *but* eat — at least that's the way they see it —

DAISY. I've never said they can't go into the spare rooms upstairs, I've never said that, although now you mention it they couldn't because of course Jenny's in Dick's and now Matthew wants one to himself he's in Benedict's and

Benedict's lying down in Henry's and they'd wake him, wouldn't they Jasper?

MARIANNE. Well, of course, if Benedict needs to lie down — Anyway, they've got to have it now because poor old Henry's got to go and see Mrs O'Killiam —

DAISY. Who?

MARIANNE. — and it's all getting a bit — so, for goodness' sake darling, let's give them their tea at home —

DAISY. What, take them home, you can't take them home, I've sliced three loaves and buttered the slices, no no, you can't take them home you know, not without their tea, can they Jasper?

HENRY. But Nanty, if it's asking too much of you —

DAISY. If they need their tea now, let them have it now, by all means, I'll go and see to it straight away — here, Henry, you'd better give me that — (*takes the towel away from him*) and I'll put these in the back-kitchen — (*as she goes*) and oh, by the way, if Nindy wants her pot you'll find it sluiced in the down-lavatory.

*There is a pause.*

MARIANNE. Golly, well we seem to have put our foot in it again, don't we darling?

HENRY. I think she's got one of her headaches, darling, and a bit tired with it. You know.

MARIANNE. Oh. Oh well, poor old Nanty — I'd better go and keep the peace.

HENRY. No, I'll go darling, you relax and have a jaw with Daddy, you haven't had a proper one yet.

MARIANNE. Well, you *are* marvellous at dealing with her, I'll take over later, when you've got her back under your thumb.

HENRY. Righto, darling. (*Goes out through the arch.*)

MARIANNE. I don't know what it is about Nindy's pottie that brings out the worst in Nanty, do you Gramps, all that fuss over the soup tureen last week and then hiding it in the kitchen cupboard did Henry tell you about that Gramps, before lunch when she thought I'd forgotten it again, not that I hadn't learnt my lesson though what could be less offensive

than a toddler's wee, I mean I wasn't going to dish it out as
soup or anything — Oh I'm not getting at Nanty, Gramps —
Gosh I'm just as bad as she is sometimes. I know I am, why
just the other afternoon I had quite a funny moment, well
it wasn't funny at the time, oh it was the usual sort of
thing Gramps, Nigel and Simon were quarrelling in the cubby-
room over whose turn on the skate-board I think it was while
I was dishing up their six o'clocks, horlicks for Nigel and Tom
and Piers, ovaltine for Simon and Nindy and me, and I was
stirring away as usual, out of the corner of my eye I caught
myself watching them at it, Simon had the skate-board hugged
to his chest and Nigel trying to struggle it out of his arms, and
on their faces there were such expressions, but oh,  perfectly
normal, Gramps, golly! (*Laughs.*) They were just being
children, humans, that's all, but still I caught myself, I was the
horrible one, caught myself wishing they were, all of them,
Tom and Piers and Nindy too, though Piers and Tom were
upstairs quite innocent in front of childrens' television for all I
knew and Nindy was sitting in her highchair humming bubbles
out quite nicely and for all I knew feeling quite nice, but all of
them, I wished all of them, this one too, isn't it a horrible
Mums? (*To her belly.*) Oh, it was just a flash, Gramps, just
an out of the corner of my eye thing, deep and midnight stuff,
but it had never happened before, you see Gramps, so of
course now I keep remembering it, it pops in and out when I
least expect it, that I actually wished — oh, I know I'm not
like that really, or the house would be full of corpses, (*laughs*)
all I mean is that it's a jolly funny business, life and parent-
hood and all that — and if my Henry weren't around now that
this thought's taken to popping in and out more and more and
sometimes all the time even — I might be in danger  of going —
well, a bit potty. (*Laughs.*) What do you think, Gramps?

MARGARET *enters. She is smoking.*

MARIANNE. Oh hello Maggie!

MARGARET *smiles.*

But I say, you haven't been out in this have you?

MARGARET. Yes.

MARIANNE. Golly, why?

MARGARET. Oh — for a walk.

MARIANNE. Gosh, didn't you get wet?

MARGARET. I took shelter in a 'phone box.

MARIANNE. Oh. How did you get back?

MARGARET. In a taxi.

MARIANNE. Gosh, that was lucky, how did you get hold of one?

MARGARET. I telephoned for it.

MARIANNE. Oh, of course. Not lucky then, just jolly sensible (*laughs*).

MARGARET. Do you know where Ben is?

MARIANNE. No — oh, yes — upstairs, didn't Nanty say Gramps, having a snooze.

MARGARET. Oh (*makes to go off*).

MARIANNE. Why don't you let him get on with it, as he probably needs it from what Henry says — I mean, it's such a long time since we've seen each other and I'm longing to hear all about your success, aren't we Gramps?

*MARGARET hesitates.*

Come on then!

*MARGARET. sits down.*

Jolly good! Now — now then tell us all about your — whoops! (*Little pause.*) Whoops! (*Little pause.*) And again! He still thinks we're footering about on the Piece with Henry and the boys — and a hefty kick — and a hefty kick — he's developing too, aren't you? (*Looks down, pats her stomach.*) I just realized the other day that that's why I always assume my babies are he's, even Nindy, they've all had such hefty kicks, even Nindy (*laughs*) although Tom was the worst, I honestly think he decided to boot his way out, while Nigel was a bit more like a clog-dancer Henry used to say (*laughs*).

*There is a pause.*

MARGARET (*as if making an effort*). And which would you prefer this time?

MARIANNE. What?

MARGARET. Boy or girl?

MARIANNE. Do you know, I really don't mind, Maggie. I mean, I suppose a sister for Nindy would be convenient. At least for Nindy. But then so would another brother for Nigel, Simon

Tom and Piers. Or a sister for Nigel, Simon, Tom and Piers, come to think of it. Or a brother for Nindy. Not that *they've* given it a thought one way or another, and Henry says he'll take what comes as usual, and Gramps hasn't expressed any views either way, have you Gramps, so I'll settle for my routine, run-of-the-mill eight pounder thank you very much God, if you know what I mean (*laughs*).

MARGARET. I think so. You incline towards a baby, and you have a strong preference for either sex.

MARIANNE. Yes. (*Little pause.*) I really shouldn't make such a display, should I?

MARGARET. I don't see how you could help it.

MARIANNE. (*laughs*). No, that's true enough. Anyway, enough of babies! I was saying to Henry on our way here this morning that the few times you and I have had a proper natter it's really only me nattering away about the one I'm in the process of having or the ones I've already had and you have to go through the same old motions and ask the same old boring questions, and this time I wasn't going to let you, especially with so much to talk about yourself, I mean blossoming virtually overnight into a famous writer and tele-person even, golly, you must be jolly chuffed!

MARGARET. Well, um —

MARIANNE. No honestly, I'd be swollen with pride, wouldn't I Gramps! And what have the reviews been like, I've scarcely seen any.

MARGARET. Oh. What are called mixed.

MARIANNE. Jolly good, eh Gramps? One of the ones I read was very nice. It said you were like a scalpel, gosh (*laughs*) I think it was meant to be nice, anyway.

MARGARET. That was *The Times*.

MARIANNE. Was it, you read them all then, do you, I don't know how you could bear to. I mean the bad ones. If there were any.

MARGARET. I'd rather read them myself than have them read out to me by friends.

MARIANNE. You're absolutely right, anyway what does it

matter what they say, it's been a great success, hasn't it, and
I'll bet that infuriates them.

MARGARET. Who?

MARIANNE. The ones who were snide and snarky, there was one
I came across made me absolutely livid!

MARGARET. Oh. *The Guardian.*

MARIANNE. No, it wasn't *The Guardian*. Could it have been
*The Telegraph*?

MARGARET. No.

MARIANNE. Oh, that was a good one, then?

MARGARET. They didn't review it.

*There is a pause.*

MARIANNE. Anyway, as long as *you* think it's good, that's
what counts, isn't it Gramps?

MARGARET. Thank you. (*Lights another cigarette.*) And have
you read it yet?

MARIANNE. Oh gosh, yes, haven't I said?

MARGARET. I had the impression you called out something
at lunch. As you passed the dumplings.

MARIANNE. I know, it's such a shambles, isn't it, I was just
saying to Henry that our lot must do a marvellous job of
putting you and Ben off family life (*laughs*).

*There is a pause.*

MARGARET. And what did you say?

MARIANNE. What?

MARGARET. As you passed the dumplings.

MARIANNE. Oh — oh golly, nothing profound, knowing me.
Just the usual congratters, I expect.

*There is a pause.*

MARGARET. Did you enjoy it?

MARIANNE. Oh — oh, now I've got to be careful not to plonk
my great foot in it, but to be honest I can't say I actually
*enjoyed* it, Maggie, I didn't know you wanted me to, I mean
let's face it, it isn't just a jolly good snorter of a read, like the

usual stuff I get my nose into, for one thing you have to be on your toes all the time, but I admit I've done my share of boasting about our being fellow-sisters-in-law, especially after that T.V. thing.

MARGARET. I'm glad you got something out of it.

MARIANNE. Of course we always knew you were brainy, but not so devastatingly brainy, eh, Gramps? The way you conjured up all those weird people and being so — so ruthless and — and devastating about the whole bunch of them. Am I being very feeble?

MARGARET. You found them weird, did you?

MARIANNE. You and old Ben don't actually *know* types like that, do you?

MARGARET. Yes, actually.

MARIANNE. Then no wonder you put them in a book, that's where they belong, isn't it Gramps? Whoops — he's at it again! (*Laughs.*)

*There is a pause.*

But tell me, how long did it take you to write, I can never remember when you started, but you seem to have been at it for years.

MARGARET. Two.

MARIANNE. Years?

MARGARET. Yes.

MARIANNE. Golly!

MARGARET. From conception to delivery.

MARIANNE. Gosh!

MARGARET. I know. Especially when you think what can be turned out in nine months.

MARIANNE. What do you —, oh, I see! (*Laughs.*) Oh, but anyone can produce one of these, can't they — or is that what you meant?

MARGARET. No, I think I meant — (*Stops.*)

MARIANNE. What, Maggie?

MARGARET. Oh — merely that we're very different people.

MARIANNE. Who, you and I, you mean? Well, I'll say we are! (*Little pause.*) Although when you think about it we're only different because you're brainy and I'm not, otherwise we're at least women, after all, aren't we?

MARGARET. Which amounts to what? That we've both got wombs for breeding and breasts for feeding but we're under no obligation to use what brains we've got for thinking.

MARIANNE. Yes, I know, but isn't it awful how they rust over if we don't.

MARGARET. Which?

MARIANNE. What?

MARGARET. Which rust over, our wombs, our tits or our brains?

MARIANNE. Oh, I was thinking of myself, so I meant brains of course. But perhaps all three when you put it like that.

*There is a pause.*

MARGARET. (*lights another cigarette, puffs at it, looks at* MARIANNE). Actually, my reproductive organs work with regulation efficiency. |

MARIANNE. Oh. Oh, well jolly good, eh Gramps?

MARGARET. Otherwise I wouldn't have needed two abortions.

MARIANNE. Oh. Oh, I didn't know.

MARGARET. I know.

MARIANNE. I'm sorry.

MARGARET. What for?

MARIANNE. Well, if I've been clumsy.

MARGARET. I don't think you've been at all clumsy. I had the first when I was nineteen, to prevent an unwanted baby — by an unwanted middle-aged school-teacher.

MARIANNE. I suppose somebody might have wanted him though, mightn't they?

MARGARET. His wife didn't, when he tried to go back to her.

MARIANNE. I meant the baby. Because of all the people desperate to adopt, you know.

MARGARET. Yes, I do know. But I wasn't prepared to be their beast of burden. The second was Benedict's, two years ago.

MARIANNE. You really don't have to tell us about it, does she Gramps?

MARGARET. Oh, I don't mind.

MARIANNE. But I do rather, I'm afraid.

MARGARET. Really, what of? You've always been so open and free about that aspect of your life. Not that the Ben abortion's particularly interesting, I admit. But it happened to coincide with my beginning my novel, and as I didn't want a baby anyway, I wasn't going to let it muck up my creative processes, if you follow. Fortunately there's a bright lady gynaecologist in Hampstead —

MARIANNE. (*rising, takes a few steps*). Oooh-oooh —

MARGARET. What, what is it? (*Going to her.*)

MARIANNE. Sofa — sofa — Henry — quickly — ooooh — (*Collapses awkwardly on it.*)

MARGARET. Oh my God, oh my God, I'll get him — (*Goes towards the arch.*)

MATTHEW *has appeared at the french windows. He stands uncertainly watching. He enters hesitant.*

MARIANNE. (*holding* MARGARET's *arm*). No no — my leg — please rub it — quickly.

MARGARET *seizes her leg, begins to rub.*

MATTHEW. Um, if — if you see Mummy — um —

MARIANNE. No, no, the other one, the other one (*irritably*) quick — quick — rub!

MATTHEW. I'll be — um — I'll be up in my room —

*Goes out left quickly.*

MARIANNE. Oh God! God! Rub — rub!

HENRY. (*runs easily through the arch*). Ah, the old crampers, eh darling — here, let me, Maggie, I've got the trick of it — (*Takes* MARIANNE's *leg, begins to massage it expertly.*)

MARIANNE. Aaaah, aaah — (*with increasing relief*) that's it, aaah, clever old stick — there now — Golly, poor old Maggie, she thought I was going to litter right at her feet, didn't you Maggie?

HENRY. (*laughs, turns, sees* MARGARET's *face*). Are you all right?

MARGARET. Yes thank you. As everything seems to be under control I think I'll go and look at my husband.

MARIANNE. Jolly good! (*And as* MARGARET *goes out*). Not that I'd have dared, would I Gramps? Litter I mean, she'd probably have trampled on him, well, at least now we know, don't we Gramps, she's not infertile or frigid, darling, she has them killed, she sat there boasting about it, didn't she Gramps, she was horrible, quite horrible, wasn't she Gramps, so you come here for a minute, come on.

HENRY *hesitates, sits beside her.* MARIANNE *takes his arm, wraps it around her, leans into him.*

There, now I feel safe, no-one can harm us now, can they, we won't let her get you — aah — squeeze me, a little pressure, *you* know — that's right — aaah — aaah —

HENRY. Well, don't get too comfy darling, or you'll go into one of your snoozes.

MARIANNE. No, no, course I won't — course I won't — (*In a little girl's voice.*)

HENRY *strokes* MARIANNE's *hair, pushes a lock back, looks into her face. After a moment an expression of enormous sadness comes over his face. Then he looks at* JASPER, *smiles.*

DAISY *enters under the arch.*

DAISY. Oh, oh you're *both* in here now are you, no, no, it's all right, it's just that Henry suddenly vanished and there's a terrible squabble over those blasted rock-cakes.

HENRY *makes to get up.*

MARIANNE. No, you don't, you've done your stint with Nanty and you've still got Mrs O'Killiam to come —

DAISY *goes out under the arch.*

HENRY. (*lets out his sudden strange laugh*). Golly, sorry, sorry Daddy. ( *Does it again.*) — Must be — must be what they mean by *fou rire* — because actually she's not really quite as — as grotesque — Mrs O'Killiam — as somehow I'd led Marianne to believe, I mean it's true that she's thin, she was certainly off her food, from depression, really terrible

depression, but her face — her face is — rather touching,
delicate and there's something in her eyes, behind the fatigue
and giving up — rather — well, rather lovely, haunting — she
touches one, you see, in her despair. I don't know why I led
Marianne to believe, even right at the beginning that she was
— of course it's true her boys are brutes, that's certainly
true and — and they like to catch cats you know and tie
plastic bags around their heads — and the little girl, well
she's not a hydrocephalic but she does have adenoids that
give her face a swollen — from time to time — and her
husband, well it's nothing to do with an eighty-year-old,
woman, I don't know why I — I — you know how truthful
I've always been, perhaps it was simply lack of practice that
led me to — to — (laughs) he's certainly been in trouble with
the police, of course, for something to do with cars, I think it
was, and he's abandoned her and as I say she is — quite
naturally — given the way life's treated her — and — and — but
please don't believe I ever, I ever intended, planned, or wanted
to — actively wanted to — make love to her. I didn't Daddy, I
didn't. Even though she is now my mistress. (Pause.) You see,
what happened was well about a month ago I went around to
see her, and the door was open, on the latch, so I knew she
was expecting me, and so I went in. And there she was. On
the sofa. And a strange noise coming from upstairs. Rather
alarming, actually, until I realized it was just the little girl
asleep, snoring — and the boys were out, doing something
hideous I suppose, anyway they weren't doing it inside — So.
So it was just her. On the sofa. Looking so defeated and —
and hopeless — and the snoring from above. And me. And she
said, oh doctor, oh doctor. She's — she's Irish you know. And
started to cry. So I went over to her and put my arms around
her, to comfort her. And she seemed to want, to expect — to
*need* me to — and — well — anyway — I did. You see, it was
something I could do, something I could give her, there being
so little one can give even those who love one, isn't that true,
Daddy, and here was something so simple, I've always found it
easy to, well — and there's always been something about her
that touched me you see — and — and afterwards she clung
to me as if — and I cuddled her and everything was — I like
to think it was peaceful for a little time, it wasn't sex, you
see, not for her either. (Pause.) I prescribed myself, if you
like. On the National Health. Anyhow that's how I tried to
look at it. (Laughs.) As I say holding her. (Little pause.) I

didn't feel guilty or ashamed, or embarrassed. Not at all. And
I massaged the back of her neck, where she gets pain, and
looked in on Carla, and discussed an operation on her
adenoids and then went home as if I — as if for once I'd been
an effective doctor. (*Smiles. Pause.*) But of course nothing
ends — nothing like that ends with the act, does it? Why
should it? Give someone valium for much needed calm and
in no time they're desperate for their calming valium, and it's
no good explaining to them — Anyway. (*Laughs.*) Now she
looks upon me as her lover. Her man. She's as possessive of me
as — well, she feels she has a right to me, as she's given me
her body, as she puts it. She is Irish, after all. And so in
return she thinks she's entitled to something from me — oh,
not just money, other than the odd pound here and there,
and who can blame her for that? But well, more of *me*.
My time. My attention. My love. And now she's taken, poor
soul, to threatening me. (*Pause.*) I have a feeling she's told
her brutes of boys. Or perhaps they've watched. Or she's
allowed them to watch — no, no, I'm sure that's unfair,
unworthy — it's just that there's a window and once I
thought I — oh, I don't know. It doesn't really matter does it?
But if I don't go around then they come around, to the
surgery — and this morning, of course, to the house — so — so —
it'll get worse. I've tried to think it through — right to the
worst end — the scandal, and I'll be struck off, I suppose, and
then what it'll mean for old Marianne and the children —
one day — and — and — then I've tried to put it in the larger
scheme, *sub specie aeternitas*, no *aeternitatis* sorry Daddy.
(*A little laugh.*) And then it struck me, you see. The real
thing. That I didn't care. I'd even quite welcome it. Because
once you do begin to look at it *sub specie* it's really all such
a pitiful charade, isn't it, or perhaps not even pitiful, merely
a charade, with none of it mattering at all in view of what
happens all over the world, every minute of the day, and when
one thinks it through that far — no, no, when *I'd* thought it
through that far I felt a tremendous relief, you see, because
then I could face the fact — the fact that I've never cared,
never, I've always really known that nothing matters, and I
remembered the night Dick was killed — when I left you that
night and went home and sat in the kitchen, the house was
breathing you know, with life, Marianne upstairs waiting for
me, children in all the rooms, another in Marianne's womb —
and Mrs O'Killiam in her loneliness also, as it's turned out,

waiting for me — and some poor devil who'd lost his eye and
his daughter in a car crash I'd been to see — and Dick dead,
Dick, and I didn't care, not about any of us, not about
Marianne or Tom or Piers or Nigel or Simon or Nindy or the
unborn or any of the Mrs O'Killiams anywhere or you here
mourning the only one of us you loved — and so I gave myself
a couple of jolly hard punches, Daddy, right in the face, to
make myself care about something — and then old Marianne
came down, poor old Marianne, and I looked at her and
thought, no, no, I don't care about you either, poor old girl,
and now there's Nanty with a brain tumour more than
likely so you see, Daddy, so you see, what is the point, the
point of caring for each other and loving each other when
the end is always and always the same, *sub specie*  or any way
you look at it, Daddy, do *you* know by any chance, God
given chance? (*Pause.*) Do you? And if you don't why did
you bring us into the world, how did you dare — how did you
— I'm sorry. I'm sorry to be so childish. I should probably
have asked that years ago, but if you can answer now I'd be
jolly grateful. So I'll know what to say to my lot when the
time comes. Can you, Daddy? (*Laughs, stares desperately at*
JASPER.)

MARGARET *enters from left.*

*There is a pause.*

MARGARET. Sorry. Am I interrupting?

HENRY. What? Oh good Heavens no, Daddy and I were just
having one of our jaws, weren't we Daddy?

MARGARET *lights a cigarette. Her hand is trembling.*

HENRY. I gather you and Marianne had a bit of a ding-dong,
I hope you didn't take it too — too — I know she didn't.

MARGARET. Look, the thing is, I've got to get back to London
soon.

HENRY. Oh, What a pity.

MARGARET. And I've just looked in on Ben.

HENRY. Ah. Yes. How is he? I'm afraid he might have had a
spot too much, we were reminiscing, you know what it's
like when we haven't seen each other for a bit, eh Daddy?
(*Laughs.*)

MARGARET. He's sprawled across the bed of his childhood, with his thumb in his mouth. He's making little mewling sounds at the back of his throat. He's dribbling. And he stinks of scotch.

HENRY. Oh. Well um —

MARGARET. So I gather he's been through his fit and frenzy stage, has he?

HENRY. Well. Well, perhaps he did become a little — I'm sorry, Maggie.

MARGARET. I'm not, I'm afraid. He was due for another bout, and I wanted him to have it here. I'm returning him, you see. Giving him back. Sorry. That's unnecessarily brutal. But I've had quite enough of him, and I need you to keep him here, please, until I've moved myself out of the flat and found a place where I'll be safe. Actually, my publishers have already set that side of things in motion. (*Pause.*) No doubt you think I'm being very hard. Yes. Besides, I'm not Ben's wife anymore. Let alone his nurse, surrogate mother, victim and tart on demand. I'm a writer. My first book taught me that much. Whatever you think of it. And now that I've begun a new one, I'm going to need all my wits and as much peace as I can manage. Along with the usual ration of luck and inspiration. You see. I'm sorry. I *am* sorry to take advantage. But then Henry is a doctor, so he'll know what to do. And as you're also a decent man and a loving brother I'm fairly sure you'll do it. Oh, and there's something I should tell you. As far as I can establish, his Vintross doesn't exist. At least the only Vintross I can trace is a car-park attendant at the B.B.C. And I don't know if he got on to Hugh Rhys Jones, but if he did, Hugh Rhys Jones didn't stab himself to death in a Chinese restaurant or whatever. He's merely been transferred to Cardiff. Which may amount to the same thing, of course. (*Gets up.*) I've heard there's a good clinic outside Staines. I'll get my publisher to send you its address. And of course any committal papers you want me to sign. Oh — and my apologies to Marianne — explain that I was a trifle on edge. And now I'd better get away before he makes one of his spectral recoveries. They can be rather unnerving. (*Turns left to go out.*)

BENEDICT *enters from left. He is trembling. His colour is ghastly. He walks slowly to MARGARET. Stands in front of her.*

HENRY *gets up.*

BENEDICT. It was Dick, of course. Wasn't it? Yes, it was Dick. He's just come back you see and told me so. Back, Henry, Daddy. Old Dick. Just as he used to be, twenty-five years ago. And he was wearing that smile, you'd know the smile, Henry, when we'd caught him out in one of his little meannesses, his stealings, and he'd decided to make it up. And then — then Daddy — he put his hand out towards me, as if he was going to touch me. And I said, 'Dick, Dick — ' and he turned and went. Went away from me.

HENRY. Ben — old Ben — it wasn't Dick —

BENEDICT. Yes, it was, Hen. It was, Daddy. And I understood what it was old Dick, our old Dick, Henry, had come back to tell me, Daddy. What was it like to have Dick's willy inside you, darling? Did he hold you against the dark, as I did. Did he? (*Smiles pathetically.*)

JENNY *enters through the french windows.*

JENNY. I take it he's not come back, then?

HENRY. Oh. Well actually I think Ben saw him a short while ago. Didn't you Ben?

BENEDICT. What?

HENRY. He came into your room for a moment, you were just telling us. Because that's where he's staying the night, you see. Matthew.

BENEDICT. Matthew?

HENRY. Yes, Ben. Matthew, old chap. (*Goes to him gently, takes his arm.*) Matthew, you see.

BENEDICT. Oh. Oh yes Matthew — so alike, so alike it makes the heart — heart — sorry Hen, sorry — sorry — darling. Sorry Jen. Sorry Daddy.

JENNY. Did he say anything?

HENRY. No, apparently he came in and saw — well, old Ben was having a nap, weren't you Ben, so he went away again, apparently, from what Ben was saying, didn't he, eh Ben?

JENNY. Well, that's our day together. He has to be back first thing tomorrow. Our only day together in a month and then another month until half term, and I can't go on looking for

him any more, I'm soaked through, my feet are wet and I'm
worn out, he's quite worn me out with his — of course you
realize it's deliberate, don't you, I expect you've all noticed
how he avoids me, when I so much as put my hand on his
arm he flinches, draws away from me — he loathes my touch,
you see, his mother's touch. Oh yes — yes — I'm sure you've
noticed — perhaps you want it even, do you? So that you can
see he's still Dick's son, not mine, I expect that's why you
wanted him to stay on at that school — isn't it — well, I'll tell
you one thing, he's not going back, no, he's not going back
there, with that housemaster — I hate that housemaster —
writing to you, how dare he write to you! How dare you let
him! (*To* HENRY.) Well he won't any more, you won't any
more, he's coming back home with me, to live with me where
I can watch him and guard him and look after him, I've a
right to that, if I'm going to die for him a thousand times a
day I've a right to that, I'm not going to let him end up like
Dick, no I'm not, we're never going to set foot in this house
again — neither of us! Neither of us! He's *my* son. Not *yours*!
(*Looks around at them.*) Yes, this is Dick's frump speaking.
Dick's frump! That's what you all thought of me as, you
couldn't understand how your brilliant Dick could come to
marry me, could you — but then you didn't know him, didn't
see him as I saw him, night after night, crying, or curled up —
so pathetic — but I knew it was hopeless, hopeless, nobody
could have saved him, nobody, every time he went off on that
motor-bike I knew — knew what he wanted and at the end I
almost wanted it too, yes I did, because if he couldn't find
anything in me or our Matthew to keep him then he might as
well — well I'm not letting him go like that, not letting my
Matthew go like that. I'm not. I'm not.

MARGARET (*goes to her*). Jenny — Jenny — I know what you're
feeling —

JENNY (*slaps her*). Do you? (*Laughs.*) Do you? With your nasty
mean little novel, do you think — do you think he cared for
you either, why, why you were one of hundreds, hundreds,
there was an Australian sociologist at the same time as you,
the very same time, she was called Dick's Kangaroo because
she'd hop into bed with him anywhere, even places where
there wasn't one, that was the joke about her, and his
students, Dick's lucky dips, and that furry little woman in the
bursar's office, all going on at the same time —

MATTHEW *enters through the french windows.*

*There is a pause.*

MATTHEW. Um — (*clears his throat*) — Hello Mummy.

MARIANNE. (*enters through the arch*). Ah, all here, jolly good — Nanty's seeing them around to the van, darling, and I've just potted Nindy but no luck this time, even Gramp's magic didn't work, you must have spent her last penny after lunch, eh Gramps, anyway we're all set darling, sorry we've got to leave so early, old Henry's fault for being needed as usual, but golly it was lovely seeing us all together again, eh Gramps?

DAISY (*enters from left*). I've got them all in dears, now Nindy's got the pottie and Nigel's looking after the boots and Simon and Nigel are in charge of the coats and Tom's promised not to toot the horn, but before you go dears there's something you want to tell them, isn't there Jasper, I've been thinking dear, and they have a right to know who I am, haven't they dear. We're married, you see. Jasper and I. (*Pause.*) Aren't we Jasper. There! (*Laughs.*) We knew that would surprise you. Didn't we Jasper?

*There is a pause.*

Oh, it wasn't a proper ceremony, in church and in white, with bridesmaids and bouquets or anything like that, no no, it was just a thing in an office, the most ordinary thing in the world except for a sweet old lady who played the organ, didn't she Jasper, but it was all a bit of a rush, you know, people waiting in the waiting room, and leaving as we entered, weren't there Jasper, but they have to keep at it all the time, you know — quite a little business in its way but Jasper was, well you know how he feels things, always so quick, isn't he dear? His shoulders shook and his mouth trembled, it did you know! And so distinguished with his white mane and a carnation in his button and he even cried, didn't you Jasper, and he was so ashamed because he thought he was holding them up you see — with so many to come, and probably queues forming — but I said, I told him, they're used to it you know, people crying and overcome and behaving strangely, they allow for it dear, they take it into account, they'll fit everybody in so don't you worry, and sure enough it just swung open, the door on the other side you see, not where we'd come in, but on the other side — oh so well organized — and out we went, didn't we

Jasper, out we went! And the people who'd been before us
were still on the pavement, laughing and chattering weren't
they dear and clambering into their cars, and another car
arrived, didn't it Jasper, with a new lot you see just as I said,
and then our car came up, we'd hired it especially, oh so
grand it was, shiny and black to take us home, and home we
came, didn't we Jasper, and I said as we went, there there my
love, my sweet, my darling — it's all over, it's finished, wasn't
it easy and quick, all finished at last and he said 'Rose, Rose
— ' aaaah! — and I said 'No no Jasper, I'm not your Rose my
dear, I'm your Daisy dear', and 'Oh my dear Daisy' he said,
so sweet he was — 'Oh my dear Daisy, not over, my Daisy,
but beginning my love', he was tired you see, weren't you
Jasper, quite dead you were, weren't you my dear, we'll have
children he said, to keep us going, send them forth in life,
didn't you Jasper, think of them waiting, waiting to enter,
we'll bring them forth, for life awaits them, the door will
open, we'll send them towards it — didn't you love, aaah
aaaah my darling — the door will open, we'll send them
towards it —

*During this speech and the following speeches the room is
brightening — through natural sunlight after the rain to an
unnatural brightness.*

The door will open, we'll send them towards it — the door is
open —

THE REST (*except* JASPER). We'll send them towards it.

   JASPER *is struggling, as if to rise. His eyes fixed in wonder.*

HENRY. The door will open —

BENEDICT. We'll send them towards it.

DAISY. The door is open —

ALL. We'll send them towards it!

JENNY. The door is open.

ALL. We'll send them towards it, the door is open, the door is
   open, we'll send them towards it.

   JASPER *has almost made it to his feet.*

ALL. The door is open, the door is open, the door is open!

   *Stillness.*

*A prolonged honking of the horn.*

JASPER *subsides into his chair.*

DAISY. Oh really — I did tell him not to!

HENRY. Sorry Nanty, but it's hard to resist —

MARIANNE. — Anyway Nanty, we are just off, this second, don't worry — well Jenny — (*kisses her*) and Margaret (*coolly*) and Ben (*kissing them both*) I hope it won't be so long next time because Gramps does love it when you — and old Mat — see you next hols, eh —

HENRY. (*meanwhile*). Ben, you um, well we'll be in touch and — and Maggie — um, um, take care the two of you um (*putting a hand on* BENEDICT's *shoulder, kissing* MARGARET) and Jenny my dear, now you're not to worry, everything'll be — and Mat — keep up the good work!

DAISY (*throughout this*). — aaah, what a shame you couldn't stay for tea, it was all laid you know, especially, but everything's in, don't worry, Nindy, the pottie, Nigel and Tom the boots and coats — so that's all right — nothing forgotten this time —

HENRY. And Nanty — (*kisses her*) I shan't forget about the headaches, I'll see to that straight away —

DAISY. Oh thank you dear, so sweet, and I'll keep on with the moist pads, shan't I Jasper?

MARIANNE. (*kissing her*). I hope we weren't too much for you this time —

DAISY. What, no no, of course not dear — they were no trouble, the boys and little Nindy — aaah! — You're never any trouble, are they Jasper?

*Honking off.*

MARIANNE. Well darling, mustn't keep Mrs O'Killiam waiting!

HENRY. Golly no, well God bless, God bless — and see you Daddy, as usual.

MARIANNE. Yes God bless Gramps — see you as usual.

HENRY *and* MARIANNE *go out left to the accompaniment of honking.*

*The honking stops.*

DAISY. Oooh — you see how it starts my head off — well, there we
are, at least we can have a proper grown-up tea, we adore the
little ones, don't we Jasper — but I must say they make it
difficult to have a proper grown-up — but I've kept most of
the rock-cakes for you, Matthew, I know Jenny got them for
you specially so I only allowed them half each so you can
have a good tuck-in dear, but oh that reminds me I still
haven't settled — now how much did we say it was Jenny, sixty-
six p. but of course my purse, I still haven't found — did I ask
you if you'd seen it Matthew, have you seen it dear, my
purse, small, green, in velours —

MATTHEW. (*with sudden fluency*). Your purse, gosh no Nanty,
I haven't seen any purse at all, a small green one did you say
in — well I'll certainly keep an eye out for it, it's terrible
when one loses things, I do it all the time don't I Mummy,
I hope there wasn't any money or anything valuable in it.

DAISY. Well about four pounds 85p. but it must be here
somewhere, you see it's the purse, that's what I care about, it
was a present from Jasper, years ago, wasn't it Jasper?

JENNY. (*who was watching* MATTHEW *during his speech*).
Ready for our walk, darling?

MATTHEW. Oh but —

DAISY. What, walk, but what about your tea, aren't you going
to have our tea first?

JENNY. No, I'd like to go now. And straight away darling
and together if you please — (*goes over, takes him by the
hand, tightly*) so that we can't lose each other.

DAISY. Oh well I must say — you'd have thought they'd have
waited, wouldn't you Jasper, they could have had tea first as
they're always so hungry —

BENEDICT (*during this, has gone over to* MARGARET, *has
stood staring directly into her eyes*). Ready, darling? I'm
rather anxious to get back. To give Vintross a ring. He'll want
to know how things are. And you must want to get back, too.
I know what it's like now — when you start a new one. (*Little
pause.*) Coming? (*Little pause.*) Coming darling?

DAISY. What, what do you mean — you're not going too — but
the tea's out you know — or Benedict a drink, dear — you
always like a drink before you go.

BENEDICT. Oh no, Nanty — (*Leading* MARGARET *towards the french windows.*) I've given that stuff up now virtually for good, haven't I Daddy — but we'll be back soon — We won't leave it so long before the next time, Daddy, that's a promise. (*They go.*)

DAISY. What, well that's all very well but after all the trouble I went to — and the muffins — all those muffins — and what for? What for? Lay it down on the assumption and then just clear it all away again — you see — like a housekeeper — but what about you, Jasper, how do you feel, are you all right dear, you've gone very quiet all of a sudden.

JASPER *makes a slight noise.*

DAISY. What, dear?

JASPER. The door is open!

DAISY. Dear?

JASPER. The door is open!

DAISY. Oh, you're feeling the chill again, and such a warm sunny evening now that it's rained, but of course if you're feeling the chill, I know how it goes right through you, right through your whole system — (*going to the french windows, shutting them, locking them*) there — is that better — and oh the light — we don't need the light any more now that it's light (*turns off lights*) — and my headache you know, much better now that everybody's — (*collecting the scotch bottle and glass*) not that we don't like having them of course — though they might have stayed for tea — (*as she goes out through the arch*) don't we, dear?

(*Pause.*)

*The lights continue to go down steadily, until only* JASPER *in his chair is lit. That light remains for a few seconds and then as it goes down, the sound of organ music, distantly, then swelling to fill the theatre as*

*Curtain*

# PIG IN A POKE

PIG IN A POKE was first presented by London Weekend Television in 1969 with the following cast:

| | |
|---|---|
| GRIEG | Colin Blakely |
| WENDY | Jennifer Hilary |
| STEPHEN | John Steiner |
| MRS WYCHERLEY | Joan Benham |
| MR WYCHERLEY | John Harvey |
| AMANDA | Jane Bond |
| LEARY | Donald Sumpter |
| MR HUGGLE | Clifford Cox |
| VERONICA | Meg Ritchie |
| McGONNIGAL | David Engers |

*Directed by James McTaggart*
*Designed by John Clements*
*Produced by Kenith Trodd*

## Author's Note

I wrote *Pig in a Poke* such a long time ago that I can scarcely remember the circumstances. It was my first play with the late James McTaggart, and I do remember admiring his part in the production. I only hope it works as well on the page as he made it work on the screen.

S.G.

**1. Exterior. House.** *Shots of house in various stages of being for sale and then sold.*

**Credits.**

**2. Interior. The Bedroom.** WENDY, *fully dressed, goes to the chest of drawers, opens one drawer. It is piled strikingly high with underwear. She shuts the drawer, opens the one underneath it. It is piled high with gloves. Takes out a pair, goes towards the door, stops, goes back to the chest of drawers, puts first pair back in, takes out another pair, goes out, down the stairs to the living room. Picks up a letter from the desk, on down the stairs. The kitchen door is open, get a glimpse into it. She hesitates for a moment, then goes to the door facing it. Opens it. In contrast to the rest of the house, it is just as it was when it was being inspected. She hesitates a second before GRIEG'S door, then knocks, calls out:*

WENDY. Hello, Mr Grieg?

*The door opens. GRIEG is standing in vest and jeans, a mug of tea in his hand. He nods, holds the door wider, for WENDY to pass.*

WENDY. Um, we 'phoned the builders yesterday, it seems that they can come back next week to (*glances around*) put the finishing touches . . .

GRIEG (*nods, holds up his mug*). Would you like some tea?

WENDY. Um, no thank you. Really. (*Smiles.*) So we were just wondering what your plans were? (*Puts her hand on the table.*)

GRIEG (*blandly*). Thank you.

WENDY. Um, I mean, you said something about leaving?

GRIEG. Yes?

WENDY. Do you know when exactly? Because then we could tell the men when they could come in, precisely.

GRIEG. Soon. (*Takes a gulp of tea.*)

WENDY. But you don't know more definitely than that? (*More sharply, lifts her hand up, blinks, looks quickly down at her glove, which is covered with a stain.*)

GRIEG. No. I haven't finished here yet.

WENDY. Finished what?

GRIEG *shrugs.*

WENDY (*after a pause*). Only you *did* say that you'd be gone (*laughs pointedly*) and we were rather banking (*stops, looks at him*). But it will be soon?

GRIEG *smiles, little pause, then turns, goes into the kitchen. WENDY watches in confusion. He comes out holding a pair of secateurs and a cloth, puts the mug down and begins to wipe at the secateurs.*

WENDY. It will be soon?

GRIEG. Soon, yes.

WENDY. Well thank you Mr Grieg. (*Turns, goes out.*)

GRIEG *stands by the door, staring after her, Sound of WENDY on the stairs, then a stumbling noise, a sudden exclamation.*

GRIEG (*blandly*). All right?

WENDY. It's so — (*extremely irritated*) dark out here.

GRIEG. Oh, it is.

WENDY. Yes it is.

GRIEG *smiles. Sounds of WENDY going up the stairs, and cut to:*


3. **Exterior.** *Front door opens,* WENDY *steps out, clearly still irritated. Slams the door, then looks down at her glove, then at her stocking, and cut to:*

**4. Interior.** GRIEG *at the basement window, lifting back a soiled lace curtain and seeing* WENDY, *with her ankle raised, and then as* WENDY *goes down the path, out on his face, and cut to:*

**5. Exterior. A street in Hampstead.** WENDY *passes a shop window, display of lingerie, etc. She hesitates, makes to go by, then turns, goes in looking at her watch as she does so. See* WENDY *through the window, buying. She comes out of the shop carrying her purchases in chic bags.*

**6. Interior. Pub.** *The pub is fairly crowded, and cut to: the packages, on a chair, and* STEPHEN *and* WENDY *at a table. Drinks in front of them.*

WENDY. I don't believe he's got the slightest intention of going.

STEPHEN (*vaguely, he is glancing around the pub*). I suppose we'll have to do something.

WENDY. He's utterly filthy. He contaminates the whole house.

STEPHEN. No, he's not very wholesome — which reminds me, it's going to be Amanda after all. Amanda and the up-and-come-and-shove-your-face-in-it Leary. (*Looking around again*). They're meant to be meeting me here, all of them. What intrigues me is I'm sure I heard something recently about the two of them, Amanda and Leary. The question is whether it's something useful, oh, here he is. (*In a low voice. Louder.*) There you are.

WENDY *looks at him confused, then looks around. A man, young, bearded and scruffy, is standing in front of them, holding a script.*

LEARY (*North Country accent. Looks at* WENDY). Hello.

STEPHEN. Um, darling. This is Leo Leary. Wendy, my wife.

LEARY. I thought it must be, you look so alike.

STEPHEN. Is Amanda with you?

LEARY. Not quite. She's showing herself off by the door. (*Looks over towards the door.*)

*Cut to* AMANDA *who detaches herself from someone not clearly seen, drifts over to the table. She is also carrying a script.*

AMANDA. Hello. (*Smiles and nods at* WENDY.)

STEPHEN. Darling, Amanda Gracely. What do you think of it?

AMANDA *rolls her eyes, pinches her nostrils.*

LEARY (*in a flat, expressionless voice reading from script*). My dear lady, we ought to have exchanged teething rings in the registry office, or perhaps one of those ebony do-dahs in the shape of our respective throats, because that's what we spend our time sinking our respective bridge-work into. Oh Christ. A kind of Glaswegian Noël Coward.

AMANDA. Oh Christ, especially as I've just left him. So he might be in hearing-range.

STEPHEN. Oh Christ, has he turned up. I'd better go and have a word. (*Gets up, goes over to the corner.*)

LEARY (*to* WENDY). What do *you* do?

WENDY (*shrugs, smiles*). Exist.

LEARY. If you ask the house-fly the meaning of its existence, it would soon cease to exist.

AMANDA (*to* LEARY). What's the meaning of your existence? (*Little pause, smiles.*) Now how long do I have to wait? (*to* WENDY.) We're all thanking God Stephen's on this.

LEARY (*neutrally, looking at* WENDY). Yes, he seems to have got it all.

WENDY. He thinks you're both going to be marvellous. Actually, um, (*gets up, picks up her bags*)I've got to go. (*Little pause.*) Goodbye.

*Shot of her crossing the room, with her bags, towards* STEPHEN. *Seen from* LEARY's *point of view.* STEPHEN *is talking to a small man, carrying a briefcase. Then cut to the man —* McGONNIGAL, *the author, talking.*

McGONNIGAL. No, I've seen him once or twice in those North Country things, where he falls down drunk or gets into punch-ups, but I'm just wondering if he's going to catch the style, I mean, he looks a bit short on that.

STEPHEN. Oh, he's thoroughly grotty, but it doesn't matter because (*smiles*) *I've* got the style. And it's covered far worse

than him. But you don't have to torment yourself by turning
up at readings, rehearsals, etc. if you don't want — oh, hello
darling. You off? (*As* WENDY *nods.*) I'm just having a word
with our author, the one man we can't do without. (WENDY
*nods, smiles.* STEPHEN *bends forward, slightly self-consciously,
they kiss.*)

*Cut to* LEARY *watching as* WENDY *goes to the door, and then
to* STEPHEN *looking at* LEARY *with a knowing little smile, and:*

**7. Interior.** *A small, cramped office. Three desks. Telephone on
one of the desks. Behind this desk a middle-aged man is sitting.
He is plump and bearded. Come in on his face.*

MR HUGGLE (*tugs at his beard*). Um . . . . haye you done
anything like it before?

WENDY (*voice over, not yet seen, slight rustlings*). Well, you
know, just standing on street corners — and shaking my tin.
(*Laughs awkwardly.*) And then once at Oxford I was driven out
in a, well, sort of bikini thing. (*Long pause as* MR HUGGLE
*nods, waits.*) Well, you know, standing on a taxi and saluting
and (*laughs*) caught coins. (*Another pause.*) But still, (*voice
earnest*) it was *for* something, I suppose . . .

MR HUGGLE. Well, we're for something. I expect Gwen's told
you. (*Solicitously.*) Do you mind muck?

WENDY (*cut to her face for the first time. She is sitting opposite
the desk, her legs close together, the chic bags, from which the
rustlings, on her lap, and her hand pressed down on top of the
bags*). No, really. (*Leans forward, more rustlings.*) I'd love to
try it. (*Very intensely.*) I really want to. I mean, there are so
many people who need, well, help.

MR HUGGLE (*worried*). Yes, yes, there are.

*Cut to:*

**8. Interior. Kitchen.** *Carry* WENDY's *face over immediately from
the last scene, but bent, absorbed. Then down on various articles
from the carrier bags spread out. Picks up a pair of knickers, the
bra, her expression odd, the telephone rings. She gives a start, as*

*if coming out of a trance, picks the telephone up. (It is fastened to the wall.)*

WENDY. Hello. (*Little pause.*) Sorry, who? Oh — (*carefully*) Hello. Yes, of course I do, we met at lunch-time, you're in Stephen's play. Stephen's not back yet. I'm afraid, the last time I saw him was with you and Amanda, shall I get him to — (*Pause.*) No, I'm afraid that's um, I can't. (*Little pause.*) No, I'm sorry, I don't think it would be a good idea. Goodbye.

*Puts the telephone down, looks at the underwear, picks up the bra and pants, suddenly turns her head sharply. GRIEG's face at the door, as he passes. He smiles, goes on down the corridor. WENDY shoves the underwear into the carrier bag and turns determinedly to the stove, and stirs something in a saucepan.*

**9. Dining room adjoining the kitchen.** *The table with the wine bottle on it, remains of a consumed meal also on it.* WENDY's *father is at the head of the table.* WENDY *beside him.* WENDY's *mother sits opposite, but in fact closer to* STEPHEN *at the other end. There is a slight gap, in other words, between the two couples.* STEPHEN *is smoking a cheroot.* MR WYCHERLEY *has in his mouth a large, unlighted cigar. But comes in first on* STEPHEN *speaking.*

STEPHEN. The trick is to keep them on the boil for as long as I need them, for instance, I was telling Wendy, Leary had or might still be failing to have or would like to get out of something or other with Amanda and it's part of my job to find out exactly what and use it in the performances. The author on the other hand just haunts around hoping to be noticed, which he politely isn't, which is also part of my job, in other words it's a matter of oiling here and jarring there and hoping it'll turn into a — (*gestures*) — something chemical.

MRS WYCHERLEY. Darling Stephen, (*include in this exchange* MR WYCHERLEY's *handsome and cynical face*) you're terribly good at that, it must be nice to do it to such glam people.

STEPHEN. They're the most boring people in the world, simply the most boring. Absolutely unreal.

MRS WYCHERLEY (*as* WENDY *and* STEPHEN *exchange little private smiles*). Oh, don't say that, just like everybody else you mean?

STEPHEN. Oh worse, much worse, aren't they darling?

WENDY. Are they, darling? (*Innocently.*)

STEPHEN. Yes, they really are.

MRS WYCHERLEY (*with an air of triumph*). But I thought they were all meant to be so camp. (*Daringly.*)

WENDY (*lights her father's cigar during this*). All right then? (*In a low voice.*)

MR WYCHERLEY (*pulling on cigar*). All right then. (*In a low voice.*)

STEPHEN. Oh some of them are. Camply boring. Which is worse than butchly boring.

MRS WYCHERLEY (*her eyes go to* WENDY *and* MR WYCHERLEY, *away again*). The only thing is Stephen, I do hope it's not going to be one of those grubby pieces about illigits, and disinfectants and hospitals and coloured what-nots, don't you, darling?

MR WYCHERLEY (*to* WENDY). I pass.

WENDY. I should think you do.

STEPHEN. Oh no, it's going to be terribly stylish. I've promised.

MR WYCHERLEY (*abruptly*). How's your sitting tenant?

STEPHEN. What? (*Glances at* WENDY.) Grieg? Yes, well actually he's still sitting. (*Little pause.*) Really, he's quite a character, in his way.

WENDY. He's an extremely filthy character, and so is his way.

MRS WYCHERLEY. There you are, just like one of your plays.

MR WYCHERLEY (*with quiet authority*). I'd get rid of him, if I were you. You could always buy him out.

STEPHEN. Yes. (*Nods, glances at* WENDY.) Anyway, we'll think of something.

*There is a pause.*

MRS WYCHERLEY. What is exactly butch, darling?

*Cut very directly to:*

STEPHEN *full shot, in an apron, wiping a dish, and beside him* MRS WYCHERLEY *washing up, and then, through the open door, from* STEPHEN's *point of view, shot of* WENDY *and*

MR WYCHERLEY, WENDY's *hand over* MR WYCHERLEY's, *her voice very low and intimate.*

WENDY (*just heard*). You're looking very well.

MR WYCHERLEY. Am I?

*Come in on:*

WENDY. Pleasingly prosperous.

MR WYCHERLEY. But I expect I'm due to lose a little weight. How much?

WENDY. Terribly little, daddy. Three hundred pounds? For the decorators and other thieves.

MR WYCHERLEY. I'll make it four, on condition that this isn't the last time. It'll be in the post tomorrow. (*Stares at* WENDY, *smiles.*) All right, then.

WENDY. All right then. (*Smiles.*) Butch.

STEPHEN (*puts his head through the door*). Darling, is there another drying-up cloth?


**10. Interior. The Bedroom.** WENDY *comes into the bedroom, picks up the carrier bag, as from below sounds of Vivaldi. She opens the bag, peers in. Takes out a couple of garments, looks at herself in the mirror over the bed. Suddenly the Vivaldi stops, sounds of a door opening, closing,* WENDY *thrusts the stuff back into the bag, puts it down by the bed, begins to unbutton her blouse as* STEPHEN *comes in. He looks at her.*

STEPHEN. I didn't hear you come up. (*He is carrying his briefcase. He opens it, looks in. Little pause.*) You haven't told me.

WENDY. What?

STEPHEN. What he said.

WENDY. About what?

STEPHEN. About the — you know — loan? (*Turns around.*)

WENDY. Oh. (*Little pause.*) There'll be a cheque in the post tomorrow.

STEPHEN. Oh? How much.

WENDY. Three hundred.

STEPHEN (*clearly slightly disappointed*). Great. (*Shuts the briefcase.*) He's sending it to you?

WENDY. I'll make another one out to you. Now, if you want.

STEPHEN. O.K. (*Stares at her, smiles, comes over, sits down at her feet.*) Are you all right, then?

WENDY. Perfectly.

STEPHEN (*smiling knowingly up at her*). And what about Hump-them-as-soon-as-look-at-them Leary?

WENDY (*slight pause*). Leary?

STEPHEN. He didn't phone?

WENDY. Why should he?

STEPHEN. It's his method — or so I gather, from bits of gossip and pieces of rumours.

WENDY. Perhaps he doesn't fancy me.

STEPHEN. Oh, he fancies you all right. The real problem, though, is does he still or did he ever fancy Amanda.

WENDY. Wouldn't it be worse if the problem was me? (*As STEPHEN puts his hand on her knee, then slides it up under her skirt.*)

STEPHEN. Oh, I can handle you. At least, I'd know what was going on. (WENDY *gets up, goes across the room.*) Where are you going? (*Smiling.*)

WENDY. To have a bath, of course.

STEPHEN. Oh. (*Pulls out the bag, against which he has been pressing.*) What *is* in here? (*Fishes in, pulls out a pair of knickers.*) Mmmmmm.

WENDY (*turns, looks at them, him*). Be careful. (*Sharply.*) I don't want them crumpled.


**11. The Charity Office.** GWEN, *tall and dark, handsome, Australian accent,* and VERONICA, *small girl, strained manner.* WENDY *at the end of the desk, writing down items in a book.* MR HUGGLE *at·the other desk, is on the telephone. But come in* *on (having cut directly from* WENDY's *knickers) an undefinable but filthy garment, being held by* GWEN. *Then cut to* VERONICA, *and then to* WENDY. *She looks at the garment, then looks quickly away.*

VERONICA (*matter of factly*). Men's knickers.

GWEN (*drops them on top of clothes pile at* WENDY's *foot, which she moves*). Men's knickers. C. column darling, I think. (*As* WENDY *writes.*) We ought to send them back.

VERONICA (*digging in again*). Who to? You don't think they own up, do you?

GWEN (*as another object comes out*). It *can't* be!

VERONICA. Oh, we used to get masses of those, in Kilburn.

WENDY (*looking up*) What?

GWEN. A nappy, my dear, straight, by the smell of it, from baby's bum. There isn't a column for this one — put it down under miscellaneous.

*Cut to:*

MR HUGGLE (*his voice rising to audibility*). No, no I do see that and we *are* grateful for any interest, Mrs Jellybein, but I think that a local jumble sale is the best place — a church fête — (*Little pause.*) a synagogue fête then? (*Laughs.*) Oh, I'm sorry, I didn't mean — I'll certainly try and think of somewhere to place it. Goodbye.

VERONICA. What was it?

MR HUGGLE. A bone-china tea-set. In shards, I suspect. (*Watches as* VERONICA *pulls out another garment.*)

VERONICA. Vest.

GWEN (*to* WENDY). You'll have gathered by now that we're the most chi-chi tip in town. (*Takes the garment from* VERONICA, *drops it in one of the piles at* WENDY's *foot.*)

VERONICA. They mean well.

GWEN (*take in* MR HUGGLE, *sitting with his hand to his forehead*). What would we get if they meant badly then?

MR HUGGLE (*stands up, clears his throat*). I've got to go and chat up a lady who's talking cash, um, Veronica, would you mind coming along?

VERONICA *gets up, slightly self-consciously, goes out, followed by* MR HUGGLE, *who turns, nods at the other two, closes the door. There is a silence.* GWEN *picks up another piece of clothing, throws it on to one of the piles.*

GWEN. He's married, the poor sweeties.

WENDY. Oh.

GWEN. They probably have to make do with the back of his van.

**12. Interior. The first floor rooms.** *Furnished, decorated very elegantly. The Hi-Fi set is on, a Barcelona chair, on which* STEPHEN *is sitting, smoking a cheroot. He is wearing his dark glasses, perched on the end of his nose. He has his briefcase on his lap, and is doing some blocking on a square of paper. He puts the briefcase down, gets up, nodding his head slightly in time to the music. The camera follows him, across the hall, up a few stairs, goes into a door, glimpse of an extremely elegant little lavatory with a rug on the floor, little stick of deodorant, a stool beside the lavatory with a book on it. Shuts the door, little pause to music, luxurious flushing sound, comes out, nodding his head to the music, waits as it comes to climax, conducts the last few bars, brings arms down in a majestic sweep as the music stops, then turns the handle of the bathroom door. Pushes. The door doesn't open.*

STEPHEN. Darling? (*Waits. No reply.*) Darling?

*Puts his ear to the key-hole, tries the door again, faint gurgling-water sounds from within. From below the music starts again. He turns around, goes down, enters the living-room.* WENDY *is turning away from the Hi-Fi.*

Oh there you are. (*Slightly apprehensive, goes to his arm-chair, sits down, picks up his brief-case and blocking paper.*) Where've you been?

WENDY (*sardonically*). Washing-up.

STEPHEN. Oh. (*Little pause.*) Sorry, I'm just working out my campaign to keep Amanda's tits, Leary's profile and McGonnigal's camera instructions off screen.

*Bends over the paper, and shot of him from* WENDY's *point of view. She gives a little smile at him. Goes over to the book-case.* STEPHEN *looks up towards her. Licks his lips slightly. She takes a book down, goes towards the door, followed by* STEPHEN.

STEPHEN (*slightly*). Where are you going?

WENDY. To have a bath. (*They look at each other.*) You get on with your campaign in peace. (*Calmly. Goes out.*)

STEPHEN *stares at the door, then looks down at his paper, slowly begins to move his head to the music, and cut to:*

**13. Interior. The bathroom door.** GRIEG *comes out, fully dressed, his hair slicked back, looking unnaturally groomed. Hears a sound above, looks up.* WENDY, *in her pants and bra, comes down the stairs, as* GRIEG *steps back into the bathroom. She goes past the door, into the living-room.*

**14. Interior. Living-room.** STEPHEN *looks up as* WENDY *comes in, smiles at her, pretends to look down at his paper again, then looks up covertly as* WENDY *goes to the book-case, puts book back, runs her hand along the shelf. He stares at her, and cut to* GRIEG, *at the door, staring impassively at* WENDY. WENDY *moves along, looking at book titles.*

STEPHEN. What are you looking for?

WENDY. Nothing really.

*This seen from* GRIEG's *point of view, then cut to* WENDY *as she takes down a book, looks at* STEPHEN, *who stares back at her, transfixed. She turns, goes to the door.* STEPHEN *watches her, then frowns, runs the dark glasses up and down his nose, bends over the paper. Cut to* WENDY *going up stairs, from* GRIEG's *point of view a few steps down the next flight.*

WENDY (*voice over from above*). Stephen! (*More shrilly.*) Stephen!

STEPHEN (*comes running out of the living-room*). What? (*In a panic.*) What? (*Runs up to the bathroom.*)

WENDY. Look at it. Just look at it!

STEPHEN (*also voice over*). Christ!

*Cut to:*

WENDY (*coming out of the bathroom, her face set, goes back upstairs to the bedroom, comes out again almost at once*). Go down and have it out with him. The pig.

STEPHEN (*comes out of the bathroom, hesitates*). He's gone out.

WENDY. How do you know?

STEPHEN. I heard him.

WENDY *turns, goes back to the bedroom.* STEPHEN *goes into the bathroom. She comes\out again almost at once.*

WENDY. That's the limit, when he starts leaving his scum in our bath for me to sit in.

STEPHEN, *unseen, mutters something.*

What? (*Shrilly.*)

STEPHEN *comes to the door, holding package of Vim.* WENDY *turns, stubs her toe.*

Ooooh! Christ! (*Limps into the bedroom, muttering viciously.*)

STEPHEN. You all right, darling? (*Stands for a moment, then goes back into the bathroom.*)

*Cut to:* GRIEG. *He turns, goes down the stairs. Then cut to:* WENDY, *she is sitting on the edge of the bed, her hands clapsed between her knees.* STEPHEN *comes into the room. She looks up qt him blankly.*

STEPHEN. I've got it all off.

WENDY. I spend the day among filthy garments worn by filthy people, and I come back home to find I'm expected to sit in a filthy bath.

STEPHEN. Darling, don't be depressed. (*Goes over to her, kneels down in front of her.*)

WENDY. Why not?

STEPHEN (*shrugs, smiles*). It makes *me* depressed when you're depressed.

WENDY. Does it?

STEPHEN. Yes, it does.

WENDY (*smiles, a ghastly radiant smile*). Does it make you radiant, when I'm radiant?

STEPHEN (*stares up at her, gets up*). Thank you. (*Coldly.*)

WENDY. That's all right. (*Little pause.*) Daddy warned us.

STEPHEN (*after a little pause*). That's true. And very constructive. He didn't actually tell us how to go about it, though, did he? Except to buy him off with money we haven't got.

WENDY. We could always borrow it from him couldn't we? (*Sarcastically.*)

STEPHEN. What the hell's the matter with you? (*Slight shrill.*)

WENDY (*looks at him*). Is it really so hard for you to understand? I just don't like the way that pig is turning our house into his personal trough. He makes me feel sick. Can't you understand that? Can't you really? Can't you really understand that? (*Glares at* STEPHEN.) Also you didn't hear him go out. You were just fobbing me off because you're too nice or something to go down and do anything about it.

STEPHEN. I *did* hear him go out, excuse me.

WENDY (*suddenly calm, shakes her head*). You did not.

STEPHEN (*slaps his arm against his side, shakes his head*). I *did* hear him go out.

WENDY *stares at him, smiles, shrugs.* STEPHEN *turns, goes to the door, flings it open. Follow him down the stairs, running. Come to the bottom hall as* GRIEG *advances up it, dressed to go out.* STEPHEN *does a sort of jig backwards and to the side, to let* GRIEG *pass.* GRIEG *waits calmly.*

STEPHEN. Ooooops, sorry. (*Gives a little laugh.*)

GRIEG. That's all right. (*Goes on down the hall.*)

STEPHEN *goes into the kitchen,* GRIEG *goes out,* STEPHEN *reappears, goes up the stairs and cut to:* WENDY *sitting on the edge of the bed.* STEPHEN *stands at the bedroom door, then comes in.*

STEPHEN (*triumphantly*). I told you. He's gone out.


**15. Interior. Morning.** WENDY *comes down the stairs, into the hall, dressed to go out. She stands before* GRIEG's *door, hesitates,*

*then opens the door, looks down the stairs, shuts the door, turns.
GRIEG is just coming through the front door. She glances at
him quickly, then goes into the kitchen, as if she hadn't seen him.
Goes to the sink. Stiffens slightly, turns around. GRIEG is
standing at the kitchen door.*

GRIEG. Looking for me?

WENDY (*slight hesitation*). Um, oh, Mr Grieg, good morning,
yes, I was just wondering, did my husband speak to you before
he went this morning? (GRIEG *shakes his head*.) Oh. (*Little
pause.*) I know he wanted to. (*Little pause.*) About the bath,
actually. (GRIEG *tilts his head enquiringly*.) Yes, my husband
and I (*stops in recognition*) we just feel that the bath isn't in
your part of the house, frankly.

GRIEG (*nods*). You feel that?

WENDY (*very sharply*). So if you don't mind, could you *not* use it
future without at least asking us first and would you also do us
the favour of cleaning it out afterwards *if* it *is* all right for you to
use it, please. (*Long pause.*) Is that understood?

GRIEG (*nods*). Yes, I understand that.

WENDY. Good. Thank you.

*Turns to the sink, turns on the tap, come in on her face, the
tap running. She picks up a cup and saucer, holds them under
the tap, on her face an expression of tension. She turns the tap
off, as she does so she gives a jump, her eyes widen. Continues
to stare ahead as sound of footsteps crossing the floor.*


**16. Interior. The Rehearsal Room.** *Come in immediately on
STEPHEN, observed from the door, back to camera. He is
making gestures with his arms and hips, very effeminate. LEARY
and AMANDA are in front of him, making them back to him.
Various people scattered about, drinking coffee, reading.
McGONNIGAL is seated at a large table by the wall, writing into
an exercise book. Then WENDY moves forward into camera,
uncertainly. Steps sideways, sits down some distance from
McGONNIGAL. He looks at her, nods and smiles in recognition.
She nods back, watches intensely. STEPHEN has taken AMANDA
by her shoulders and is doing his effeminate dance with her.
LEARY comes over to WENDY, sits down beside her.*

LEARY (*in a low voice*. I suppose Stephen asked you if I'd 'phoned?

WENDY (*staring straight ahead*). Yes.

LEARY. And did you tell him? (*In a low voice. Pause.* WENDY *remains staring ahead*.) Don't you think I've got enough style for you? (*Little pause*.) Well, Stephen's going to give me some of his.

WENDY *turns, looks at* STEPHEN, *cut to him. He circles effeminately around* AMANDA, *sees her, stops, says something to* AMANDA, *comes over*.

STEPHEN. Darling, what are you doing here?

WENDY. Can I speak to you for a minute, please?

AMANDA (*coming behind* STEPHEN). Now we can get the real story about Mr Grieg's bath.

WENDY *looks at* STEPHEN, *who smiles fleetingly, embarrassed*.

LEARY. Apparently you think some people don't rate baths.

WENDY. What? (*Looks at* STEPHEN *again*).

AMANDA. The talcum powder bit's gorgeous.

WENDY. Talcum powder?

AMANDA (*to* STEPHEN). I knew you were lying. *His* version is that your Grieg or whatever was poncing about the house in your talc and a finger-tip or two of your best scent behind the ears.

STEPHEN (*smiles falsely*). What I *actually* said was . . .

AMANDA. And Leary's furious because Yorkshire coal-miners don't get talc and scents on the National Health, or their sons don't. Or he doesn't. Or someone doesn't; anyway he's furious about it. It seems they're betraying the working classes again, and R.A.D.A. boys with surly faces, (*leans over* LEARY, *puts her arm around his neck*) doesn't it, darling?

LEARY *straightens, tries to look up into her face, says something that makes* AMANDA *tighten her expression and then, smiling, her grip around his throat.* LEARY *attempts to break free with his shoulders. After a second* AMANDA *steps away*.

WENDY (*gets up,* STEPHEN *walks beside her towards the door*). Why did you tell them about the bath?

STEPHEN. What? No reason. It was just coffee and camping-up time before we started, one invents these things, you know. (*Little pause.*) What's the matter? I mean, why aren't you at work?

WENDY (*after a pause, shrugs*). I just wanted to see you.

STEPHEN (*blankly*). Oh. Great. You all right?

WENDY. Perfectly.

STEPHEN. Actually there's so much strange sex in the atmosphere here, I'd better not walk you to the tube. I'm beginning to think the key to a sane life is to go in for charity work. Oh Christ. (*Looking past her to McGONNIGAL, who is approaching rapidly.*) Our bloody author, he's never been to bed with — (*Points a finger.*) Tim. Hello.

McGONNIGAL. Could you spare me a moment, Stephen. There are a few notes I've jotted down.

*Cut to:*

### 17. Exterior. Shop. WENDY *in lingerie shop.*

### 18. Interior. The Hall. WENDY *comes through the front door, packages clapsed tight to her chest as she struggles to get the key back into her handbag. Suddenly stares ahead. GRIEG is baring down on her. She strives to move out of the way, packages slip, a few pieces of underwear (white) scatter to the floor. She tries to crouch to pick them up. GRIEG watches, looking down at her, and cut to her face, frantic, embarrassed, as she scrambles the pieces together, stands up. GRIEG steps past her, smiles into her face, goes out. WENDY stands for a moment, then hurries blindly along to the kitchen, drops the packages on the table, still clinging unconsciously to a pair of white knickers. Stands for a moment, then goes to the telephone, dials. A little pause. The knickers still in her hand.*

WENDY. Daddy?

**19. Exterior. Garden.** *Shot of* GRIEG *working in the garden. taken from the living room. The Hi-Fi set is playing.* WENDY *at the window (*GRIEG *from her point of view, in fact). Suddenly she looks to her left,* MR WYCHERLEY *saunters easily into the garden, a cigar in his mouth.* STEPHEN *and* MRS WYCHERLEY *follow,* MRS WYCHERLEY *with a hand across her nose. They stand for a moment, talking, then* STEPHEN *gestures to the tree at the end of the garden.* MRS WYCHERLEY *looks towards* GRIEG, *who is still crouching, then goes towards the tree,* STEPHEN *in attendance.* MR WYCHERLEY *stands smoking his cigar, then glances up at* WENDY, *smiles, saunters easily over to* GRIEG, *his hands in his pockets, stands above him.* WENDY *gives a little smile, and cut to:*

MR WYCHERLEY (*after a moment, takes cigar out of his mouth*). You're Grieg? (*Smoothly.*)

GRIEG *looks up, nods, goes on with his trowelling.*

MR WYCHERLEY. And you're what is known as the sitting tenant. (GRIEG *pays no attention.* MR WYCHERLEY *smiles calmly.*) You're a good gardener, aren't you?

GRIEG. That's right.

MR WYCHERLEY. To tell you the truth, I didn't expect to find you here. There seemed to be a general impression that you were leaving.

GRIEG (*looks up at him*). And is there a general impression that I'm still here?

MR WYCHERLEY (*smiles suavely*). You taking the micky?

GRIEG *goes back to his trowelling.* MR WYCHERLEY *glances up at* WENDY, *still at the window. The music should, of course, sound in the garden throughout this.*

Or possibly conducting a piece of business. Shrewdly, eh? (*Little pause.*) For example, being unprepared to settle for less than a hundred and fifty pounds.

GRIEG (*looks up at him*). What'd I want a hundred and fifty pounds for? (*In genuine disbelief.*)

MR WYCHERLEY (*pulls on his cigar*). What *do* you want?

GRIEG. I can get anything I need.

MR WYCHERLEY. Very well. Two —

MRS WYCHERLEY (*coming up with* STEPHEN). What have *you* found?

MR WYCHERLEY. Um, I've found Mr Grieg, digging — what the dickens is that you're digging up?

*Squats down,* MRS WYCHERLEY *and* STEPHEN *now standing around the two of them. Cut to* WENDY *still watching from the window as* STEPHEN *also crouches, and then* MRS WYCHERLEY *crouches, then, as the music achieves a superbly royal flourish* GRIEG *rises, and from* WENDY's *point of view, looks up at* WENDY *as her family remains squatting in various accidentally worshipping postures, around him.*

**20. Interior. The Bedroom.** STEPHEN, *in his pyjamas, is going through the contents of his briefcase. Takes out his dark glasses, puts them on the dresser.*

STEPHEN. Um, it was all right, was it?

WENDY (*voice over*). What?

STEPHEN. Letting the three hundred run over a bit?

WENDY (*voice over*). Don't worry, no money's going to change hands.

STEPHEN. That's very decent. (*Shuts the briefcase, turns, looks for his dark glasses, puts them on, takes them off*).

WENDY (*voice over*). You're a very pretty man, very very pretty. Gwen says you're the prettiest man she ever met. Do you know you're pretty, Stephen?

STEPHEN (*after a pause, staring at her — straight into the camera, in fact*). Yes.

WENDY (*voice still over*). Are you pleased you're so pretty?

STEPHEN (*after another pause*). Yes. (*Little pause, goes over to the bed.* WENDY *is sitting on the edge of the bed, in pale pyjamas. He sits down beside her.*) Are you?

WENDY. Mostly.

STEPHEN (*puts the dark glasses down on the bedside table*). But you're prettier. (*Little pause, then thickly.*) You know I love you. (*Pushes her tentatively down on the bed.*) I do. (*Smiles pleadingly into her eyes.*)

WENDY (*looks up at him, then slowly shakes her head.*

STEPHEN. Please, darling. (*In a whisper.*) Please.

WENDY *shakes her head again, fade out, and in on* WENDY *face up on the pillow, naked, pyjamas lying across the bed.*

STEPHEN (*voice off*). A sort of therapy party. For the whole cast cum ladies and gentlemen, my idea being to get all the noise and nastiness in one place for an evening, you know? Turn it into a collective experience — a purification rite or a ritual murder for mainly, frankly, Amanda and Leary. I shall be the observer of all observed, if Leary makes a lunge at you I'll have to rethink my strategy, but if he chases Amanda all evening I'll know I've got them taped until the taping. (*Little chuckle.*)

WENDY. Why do men do that?

STEPHEN. What? (*Complacently, voice over.*)

WENDY. Come wheedling for a bit of love or body or whatever it is they think they need and have a right to, and when they've had it they lie there like — I don't know — men.

STEPHEN (*after a pause*). What do you mean?

WENDY. What I've just said.

STEPHEN (*rolls over, looks at her*). Oh darling, come on.

WENDY (*in camera, staring up*). Come on where, darling?

STEPHEN (*stares at her, aghast, then rolls back again, stares up, tight-lipped*). Thank you very much. (*Tautly.*)

WENDY. You're welcome.

STEPHEN (*after a little pause*). I thought you loved me.

WENDY. I do. (*Turns her head, looks at him, then with her finger traces the line of his nose, smiles, says flatly.*) Because you're so pretty.


**21. Interior. The Living-room.** *Party in progress. About forty guests. The Hi-Fi set playing some cool modern stuff, very low, and over it the row of voices. Visible among the guests several*

*members of* STEPHEN's *production group, take them in
generally, then transfer to a man talking to* WENDY. GWEN
*talking to* STEPHEN, AMANDA *standing aloof, with* McGONNIGAL
*unhappily beside her. She is watching* LEARY. *Then cut briefly
and tantalisingly to a shaggy head and back, to give just an
impression of* GRIEG *in a corner. Come back to* WENDY *and her
man.*

STEPHEN (*laughing boyishly, sweeping his hair out of his eyes.
There should be a little play from* GWEN, *intensification of
expression*). Well, actually I don't think he intends to join us
this evening.

GWEN. You should have asked him up. Then we could have
occupied his basement, which would have been much nicer.

LEARY. How's Stephen?

WENDY. Don't you know?

LEARY. Well, I don't suppose he handles you like the ladies and
gentlemen of the cast, does he? Wouldn't the strain show in a
bit of wife-beating, or sommat?

WENDY (*licks her lips, then with a tight smile*). Wrong class, I
think.

LEARY. Is it husband-beating down in the stylish South?

WENDY. Or sommat. (*nods.*)

WENDY *looks from* AMANDA, *who is smiling pleasantly, to*
LEARY, *whose face is suddenly set, then looks vaguely
around, sees* STEPHEN, *back with* GWEN *but smiling knowingly
towards her, then on past more guests, standing with a drink,
looking around, puzzled, then on, sees* GRIEG *by the door,
his back to her and stooping slightly.*

WENDY. Excuse me, there's somebody there I have to, um . . .
(*Walks towards* GRIEG, *determined.*)

AMANDA (*to* LEARY, *who is watching her go*). Well, what is it
with Mrs Cool-Knickers, class or sex? Or both?

LEARY (*savagely*). It's what you haven't got. What is it? (*Savagely.*)

*And cut to:*

WENDY *a few feet away from* GRIEG's *back.* VERONICA
*suddenly brushes around from in front, her face tremulous,
looks past* WENDY *blankly, sees* MR HUGGLE, *goes over to*

*him. He looks at her in concern.* WENDY *stares after them, then looks at* GRIEG, *who, turning, smiles at her. She glares at him, goes over to* VERONICA.

VERONICA. It doesn't matter. (*To an inaudible enquiry from* MR HUGGLE.)

WENDY. Did he — do something?

VERONICA *glances at* WENDY, *tears in her eyes, shakes her head, looks away.*

WENDY. He said something, then?

VERONICA *shakes her head.*

WENDY *turns, looks towards the door. It is open.* GRIEG *has gone. She walks to the door purposefully, and out, closing it behind her. Cut back to the party,* GWEN *at the Hi-Fi set,* STEPHEN *standing beside her, watching, slight smile on his face, and cut to his view of* LEARY *talking savagely into* AMANDA's *face,* AMANDA *smiling contemptuously,* McGONNIGAL *just behind them, and cut back to:*

**22. Interior. The Stairs.** WENDY *goes down them to the ground floor hall. Turns on the light, goes to the door that leads to the basement, opens it, as from above thumps of dancing feet and loud music come. Goes down to* GRIEG's *door, her face set, flings it open. Keep on her face, don't show* GRIEG.

WENDY (*controlled, smiling with the effort*). You crashed our party. (*Little pause.*) You helped yourself piggishly to our drink, which you gulped down piggishly, you insulted one of my friends, a girl who's incapable of being unkind to anyone, even a pig like you, and then you run off, like the cowardly pig you are. You'd bloody well better go straight upstairs and apologise to my friend before I get my husband and some of his friends to throw you out, sitting tenant or no sitting tenant. (*Cut to* GRIEG, *facing her, watching her impassively.*) Do-you-hear-me?

GRIEG, *after a long pause, walks towards her.* WENDY *steps aside to let him pass. He grabs her hand, jerks her inside, slams the door.*
WENDY *stumbles, nearly falls. Steadies herself against the table, stares at him.*

GRIEG (*after a long pause*). Enjoying *your* party?

*He comes over, stands close to her.* WENDY *stares at him. He puts out his hands, one on each side of her face.* WENDY *spits into his face.* GRIEG *smiles.*

WENDY. Let go of me!

GRIEG *stares into her face, his face very close. She stares back, increasingly as if mesmerised. Then he takes her hand, pulls her out of the basement door, tugs her up the stairs, very fast. She is trying to grab at something to pull herself back, he pulls her up the next flight, to the door of the party, puts his hand at the back of her neck.*

GRIEG. Now who'll you send down for *your* apology?

*Cut to:*

**23. Interior. Living room.** *Party in progress, dancing, etc.* STEPHEN *is hopping about with* GWEN, AMANDA *is leaning forward, talking into* LEARY's *face.* MR HUGGLE *and* VERONICA *are talking intensely. The door opens,* WENDY *comes in with a little stumble, straightens herself, whirls around, nobody notices.* GRIEG *is standing at the door, staring at her. There is a long pause, then he smiles, leans forward, closes the door.* WENDY *remains looking at it. Suddenly there is a slapping sound behind, a little scream,* WENDY *turns around, as if dazed.* LEARY *is holding his cheek,* AMANDA *is walking away from him. A slight hush, then* LEARY *strokes his cheek, laughter starts, slightly self-consciously,* LEARY *walks after* AMANDA. *Cut to* STEPHEN, *from* WENDY's *point of view. He looks towards her, makes a small amused face, then hops with* AMANDA *out of the picture. Someone comes up beside* WENDY, *at first not seen properly.* WENDY *looks up at* McGONNIGAL, *his face, anxious, slightly pleading and cut to:*

**24. Interior. Bedroom.** WENDY *is lying on the bed, staring up at the ceiling in her pyjamas. Her arms are wrapped around her chest. Shouts from below, crashes, laughter, then the front door slamming. Pause. Then the sound of feet, slow, heavy, on the stairs. The door opens, slowly,* STEPHEN *comes in. He walks to*

*the chair, sits down. Brushes hair away from his eyes, smiles at*
WENDY.

STEPHEN. Well? (WENDY *looks at him*.) Make what you can of
this. (*Speaks very carefully, smiling*.) They arrived together,
they had their spicy little slap-up, they left together. He came
back alone, she came back alone. He was ogling around for
something, like possibly my wife, she stood watching him from
a dark corner. He drank. She got his coat. They left together
(*Smiles*.) What do you make of this?

WENDY *stares at him*.

STEPHEN (*his smile slightly unfocussed*). Meanwhile back in the
kitchen Aussie and GWEN were running amok all over my
twelve year old P.A., and your Charity fiend with the beard
was cuddling a lady that definitely was not the bearer of his
kiddies except possibly currently, actually and frankly. He
fancies you, Leo Leary does. So observed the observer of all
observed. (*Makes a little laughing sound, stops, gets up,
smiling vaguely*.) Just a minute darling. (*Goes to the door,
opens it, turns, smiles, close-up on his face, damp and his
smile is sickly*.) Won't be a minute darling.

*Cut to* WENDY's *face as sound of his feet running down the
stairs, then as the door is flung open below, out on* WENDY's
*face*.

**25. Charity Office.** *In on* VERONICA, *sitting at the desk, going
through a ledger, her hand over her eyes. Cut to* GWEN *and*
WENDY, *seated at opposite ends of the desk, unwrapping
packages*.

GWEN (*voice over before she is seen*). Well, everyone I saw was
pissed to the newts, which is the only sign, and there was
that lovely Leary being slapped around.

WENDY *glances towards* VERONICA, *who stands up
suddenly, and with jerky movements picks up her handbag,
goes out*.

GWEN (*raises her eye-brows, shrugs*). One of her really bad days.

*Takes out of her paper a pair of baggy trousers, puts them on
the desk, as* WENDY *takes out of her paper a pair of plus fours,
puts them on the desk*.

They were having a terrible time —

*Stops as the side door opens,* MR HUGGLE *comes in. Looks towards* VERONICA's *desk.*

MR HUGGLE. Um, Veronica popped out, has she?

GWEN. Yes.

MR HUGGLE. Well, perhaps I'll just, um. (*Goes to the main door, and out. Closing it after him.*)

GWEN. Oh Christ! What you could call a —

*Main door opens,* MR HUGGLE *comes back in. He is accompanied by a small man in a black suit.*

MR HUGGLE (*going to the other door*). If Veronica — when she comes back, could you say the, um, accountant's dropped in? (*shuts the door.*)

*There is a pause.* GWEN *draws another package to her, shakes out another pair of voluminous and grubby trousers.*

GWEN. Now we're being rejected by one of those underdeveloped countries.

WENDY (*stands up abruptly*). Look, do you mind, I've got to get back, um, do you mind?

**26. Exterior. The House.** WENDY *coming along the pavement, footsteps falter, then she goes quickly up the path, unlocks the door, goes in. Goes straight up the stairs to the living-room.*

**27. Interior. Living-room.** *It's in a filthy state; glasses, bottles, ash-trays everywhere. She looks around, trance-like, steps over bits and pieces, takes off her coat, puts it on a chair, it slips to the ground. She makes a weary gesture, puts it over the chair again, looks around her. Picks up a glass, shakes her head, puts it down again. Touches her forehead, then goes to the Hi-Fi, puts on some Mozart. Goes to the garden window, looks out. Shot of* GRIEG *in the garden, sitting on a kitchen chair, reading a newspaper.* WENDY *licks her lips nervously, opens the window, steps away.*

**28. Exterior. Garden.** GRIEG *in the garden, from behind, still reading the newspaper, strains of Mozart coming down. He lowers the newspaper, looks up. Shot of* WENDY's *face, jerking away. He goes on staring. Pause.* WENDY's *face reappears, she stares straight ahead, then looks down.* GRIEG *stares up,* WENDY *withdraws her head.* GRIEG *gets up slowly, stands in the centre of the garden, music still continuing. Then shot from the window, the music very loud, looking down at* GRIEG, *looking up, then turning his head right. Keep shot from the window, looking down as* WENDY *comes into the garden, looks at him, walks towards him, stops a few feet away. This, if possible, as the first movement comes to an end.*

WENDY (*her voice heard faintly*). Pig!

> GRIEG *walks towards* WENDY. *She holds her ground for a moment, then turns, walks quickly away.* GRIEG *follows.* WENDY *begins to run,* GRIEG's *pace quickens, the garden from above now seen as empty. There is a sound from below, like a cry, then the slam of the door, then cries from within, then hold shot of the empty garden, music again in full flow, and fade out.*

> *In on:*

**29. Interior. Hall.** STEPHEN *comes into the hall, carrying his briefcase. He looks tired. Goes into the kitchen. Comes out again. Starts up the stairs.*

STEPHEN. Darling!

> *Gets to the living-room door, is about to open it, then looks up the next flight, and cut to:*
> WENDY *standing half-way up the stairs, coming down. fully dressed in a white frock, her hair done up behind her. She is wearing* STEPHEN's *dark glasses.*

STEPHEN. Hello.

WENDY (*tentatively*). Hallo,

STEPHEN. Still hung over?

> WENDY *walks down the stairs towards him, slowly and carefully.*
> STEPHEN *stands watching, smiling but slightly puzzled.*

*When she is a stair above, thus making their heads on a level,*
*he bends forward, kisses her on the forehead. Puts his hands*
*on her cheeks. She winces, just slightly. He takes the glasses*
*off, smiling.*

STEPHEN. Christ! (*One of her eyes is bruised.*)

WENDY. I walked into the door. In the bedroom. (*Bravely*
*smiling.*)

STEPHEN. Poor darling. Will it be all right? It looks ghastly.

WENDY. Yes.

STEPHEN *kisses the air close to her eye. They gaze at each*
*other for a moment, he puts the spectacles back on her nose,*
*turns, stops.*

STEPHEN. What door in the bedroom?

WENDY. The cupboard door. In the landing.

STEPHEN (*enters the living-room, in its state of chaos*). God,
what a tip!

WENDY (*follows, walking stiffly*). I'll do it tomorrow, I can't go
anywhere looking like this anyway.

STEPHEN. O.K. (*Sinks down into a chair.*) God.

*Shakes his head, then reaches out, turns on the Hi-Fi. WENDY*
*stands beside him, then walks to chair opposite, sits in it,*
*facing him.*

WENDY. How's Leary?

STEPHEN. What? Oh, hung-over and strangely absent when we
needed him.

*Smiles, touches his head, winces slightly, long pause, and on*
*the two of them facing each other amidst the debris, fade.*


**30. Interior. The Living-room, the following morning.** WENDY *is*
*in a sort of smock, a turban round her head, dark glasses on. She*
*is plugging in the hoover. She goes to the Hi-Fi, looks around her,*
*looks towards the window. Licks her lips, looks quickly away.*
*Picks up a few glasses with great efficiency, then puts them down*
*again. Walks to the window as if in spite of herself, taking off her*
*dark glasses as she does so and putting them in the smock pocket.*

*Opens the window, looks out. Then withdraws her head, turns with a look that could be disappointment on her face, jumps. Cut to* GRIEG, *standing inside the room.*

WENDY (*very controlled, touching her glasses*). Please go.

GRIEG (*walks towards her, then past her, to the window. Looks out*). Nice view.

*Cut to the garden, stay on the garden, and* GRIEG *looking down at it, as:*

WENDY. I don't care what you think of me, (*still very controlled*) because frankly and honestly what someone like you thinks isn't very important anyway, and I'm perfectly prepared to concede (GRIEG *steps away from window, out of camera which stays on the garden*) that perhaps to some extent —

*Little silence followed by squeals, sound of tussling,* WENDY's *squeals getting louder, glasses smashing, then sound of door shutting. Hold shot on garden, and:*

**31. Interior. The Basement.** *Track over* WENDY's *clothes, scattered everywhere in the semi-darkness, then to her lying on the bed in the plastic overall, her hair loose. She is staring up blankly. The kitchen door opens, right.* GRIEG *comes in, buttoning up his shirt. Picks up the secateurs, goes back towards the door.*

GRIEG. The kettle's on, I'll have mine outside. *I've* got work to do. (*This with the very faintest touch of self-righteousness.*)

WENDY *lies still for a moment, then fumbles in her overall pocket, produces the dark glasses, puts them on, stares up, and cut to:*

**32. Interior. The Hall.** GRIEG's *basement-landing door, and the front door open simultaneously.* GRIEG *and* STEPHEN *advance towards each other,* STEPHEN *does his skip and shuffle out of* GRIEG's *way, nodding, smiling at him.* GRIEG *nods impassively back, goes out.* STEPHEN *looks after him, then goes up the stairs.*

**33. Interior. The Living-room.** STEPHEN *opens the door, looks in. A shot of it in chaos. He closes the door, goes to the bedroom. WENDY is sitting before the mirror, dressed and with her hair pulled back, the dark glasses on. She looks at STEPHEN, at the door.*

WENDY. Hello.

STEPHEN. How are you?

WENDY (*shrugs*). All right.

STEPHEN. And the eye?

WENDY. Blacker.

STEPHEN (*after a pause*). What have you been doing?

WENDY. Having a bath.

STEPHEN. You went to the office today, then?

WENDY. No. (*Turns, lifts up the glasses to inspect her eye.*) You know I didn't. I was going to clear up the living-room, remember.

STEPHEN. Yes.

WENDY *goes on inspecting her eye.* STEPHEN *laughs. Little pause.*

Well . . . . . ?

WENDY *turns, looks at him impassively.* STEPHEN *shrugs.*

It hasn't been done.

WENDY (*frowns*). No. We'll have to do it tonight. (*Shakes her head at herself in the mirror.*)

STEPHEN (*stares towards her*). We're in the studio tomorrow. So. (*Smiles slightly, a martyred smile.*) I'm getting stomach tension or something or other, inevitably.

WENDY. Are you? (*Vaguely.*) Where?

STEPHEN. In the stomach. (*Looks at her reflection in the mirror.*)

**34. Interior. The Living-room.** *The glasses gone. Order restored. But come in first on WENDY's overall, and the part of the Hoover from hands down to knee level. Then the Hoover stops, and cut to WENDY, in a chair, legs hanging over the side. She is watching STEPHEN doing the Hoovering.*

STEPHEN (*still in the overall crosses to the Hi-Fi, as he does so, sniffs*). Must say, a funny smell these things have got. (*Clutching at the overall.*) I don't know how you could bear to wear it.

WENDY. It's only for when I've got something dirty to do.

*Out, and in on:*

**35. Interior. The Living-room.** *In on* WENDY. *The Hi-Fi going. Bach. Then cut to* STEPHEN *in the armchair, sitting with his feet up, his collar undone. His face has a set thoughtful expression, he is nodding his head very slightly to the music.*

STEPHEN. You know (*still jogging his head slightly*) I've been thinking. The time's come to do something final about our friend downstairs.

WENDY. Oh?

STEPHEN. I don't know, I mean I met him in the hall this evening, and it suddenly got to me. Why *should* we put up with him? It's the way he somehow gets into everything.

WENDY. I know.

STEPHEN. And how do we know what he's up to, anyway. As far as we're concerned he could be up and down, in and out, all day long. (*Little pause, jounces his head in a lively fashion to a lively piece of music.*) Know what I mean?

WENDY. Yes, I do. (*Also jouncing her head slightly, both of them doing it,* STEPHEN *extravagantly,* WENDY *demurely, as the record ends.*)

STEPHEN. Isn't that smashing! (*Little pause.*) I don't know, frankly and actually — (*Stops.*) God knows what Leary's up to, he's off somewhere or other every ten minute break, Amanda just grins Cheshire — Something very funny's going — (*Stops as music starts again. He sits listening to it, looks at* WENDY, *frowns. She reaches up slowly, takes off her dark glasses, there is a pause, her face very serious, then it breaks into a sudden, frank inviting smile. Stay on this as she licks her lips, and cut to:*)

**36. Interior. The Hall.** WENDY *goes down the hall, dressed to go out, very determined, wearing the dark glasses. Hold on the door,*

*it opens,* WENDY *comes in. Back down the hall. Opens the door
to the basement. Goes down.*

**37. Interior. The Basement.** WENDY *goes to the bed, sits down,
takes the dark glasses off, puts them down. Folds her hands into
her lap, her expression is very patient. Fade out, then in on her
sitting there as sound of door from the garden opening, and
closing, footsteps.* WENDY *licks her lips, stares with her hands
folded at the door, as it opens. Cut on her almost school-girl face,
in on her face, hair hanging dishevelled, then she raises a mug to
her mouth, sips from it. Lowers the mug, and cut to* GRIEG,
*standing in the kitchen door, also sipping a mug.*

WENDY (*with casual malice*). Your days are numbered. My
husband's decided to get rid of you. (GRIEG *pays no
attention.*) He'll knock you about and throw you into the
street bodily. (*Little pause.*) He'll think of something. He's
good with people. Jarring and oiling them. (*Pause.*) He's
only started noticing you now that you're not around so
much. What are you around so much for?

GRIEG. What's there to be around for?

WENDY (*after a moment, nods*). Thank you.

*The telephone rings distantly.* WENDY *stares up at the
ceiling.*

WENDY. That's probably him now.

GRIEG. It sounds like him.

*They listen to the telephone. It rings a few more times, stops.*

WENDY (*after a pause*). I'm going upstairs. (*Stands up, see
her from the back, her dress is open, she is carrying a bundle
of her underwear under her arm, stockings trailing down.*)
God, why are you so dirty. (*Picks up one of the magazines
from a pile, looks at it, shot of its cover, drops it back on the
chair.*) Such a pig.

GRIEG. Watch it. (*Slightly menacing.*)

WENDY (*stops, turns, looks at him. Come in on her face. Licks
her lips. Upstairs, the telephone starts ringing again. She
stares at* GRIEG, *who stares back at her. Then, in a whisper,
excited and fearful*). Pig. Pig.

**38. Interior. The Living-room.** STEPHEN *and* WENDY *as the night before, only come in on* WENDY *in dark glasses, from* STEPHEN's *point of view.*

STEPHEN. Do you still need those things? (*Voice over.*)

WENDY *nods.*

STEPHEN. I tried to get you this morning. Here and at the office. Nobody knew where you were.

WENDY. I had an accident.

STEPHEN. What? (*Cut to his face.*)

WENDY. I tripped down the stairs. (*Little pause, then looking at him very solemnly, lifts up her skirt, shows him a bruise on her thigh.*)

STEPHEN *stares at it.*

WENDY. So actually and everything I couldn't face the thought of all the grot of the office. I took the day off. (*Little pause.*) I was being naughty.

STEPHEN (*stares at her, licks his lips*). Um, Leary, um, (*Stops.*) Want some music?

WENDY *shakes her head. Smiles at him.*

STEPHEN (*gets to his feet, looks vaguely around*). Did we do the dishes? (WENDY *still smiling.* STEPHEN *staring at her as if mesmerised.*) I'd better go over my shooting script, um . . .

WENDY (*tilts her head to one side, smiles lasciviously*). Come over here. (*He goes over.*)

WENDY (*reaches up, touches his nose, presses it*). You haven't told me yet *who* is doing what to *whom*. (*Draws his hand to her and cut to:*)

WENDY *and* STEPHEN *on the living-room carpet. Clothes around them, his folded into a neat pile, hers scattered indifferently. Cut to their faces,* WENDY *is staring up, smiling. Bruise showing.* STEPHEN's *is turned into the camera, it has a slightly doped look, eye-lids heavy. Then* WENDY's *face moves off camera, stay on* STEPHEN's *as Bach begins. His eyelids open.*

STEPHEN. He's got something going all right. And it's not with Amanda. (*Eyelids begin to close again, and cut to:*)

**39. Interior.** *Come in on* WENDY's *face, she is seated on* GRIEG's *bed, hands folded in her lap. Suddenly she gets up, walks across the room, opens the door, and out. As the kitchen door opens,* GRIEG *comes in, stands, as sound above of front door closing.* GRIEG *tilts his head to one side.*

**40. Interior.** *Before the Charity Office door.* WENDY *takes a breath, adjusts her glasses, opens the door.*

**41. Interior. The Office.** WENDY *at the door, not seen, the office from her point of view.* VERONICA *most prominent, staring towards her; a handkerchief to her mouth. Behind her, two men, tough and impassive, and the accountant from the earlier scene.* MR HUGGLE, *plucking at his beard.*

GWEN (*comes up beside her, from around the other corner*). Oh, I shouldn't bother, darling, we're closing up while Mr Huggle and his Veronica accompany these gentlemen to the station, to answer some questions about the books.

**42. Interior.** STEPHEN's *figure, advancing up a long corridor with* AMANDA *just behind him, on one side,* LEARY, *on the other, and another girl behind him.* P.A.s, *ladies and gentlemen of the staff, clustered behind him. They advance into the camera, and as they pass,* McGONNIGAL *bringing up the rear, carrying his briefcase. Cut to a shot of them from behind,* McGONNICAL *making a little run to keep up.* STEPHEN *and* McGONNICAL *are in ordinary clothes, also* P.A.s, *of course. But ladies and gentlemen are in evening clothes, as is* AMANDA. *Watch the group from the back, they stop suddenly, then stand before a doorway,* STEPHEN *sitting on the desk, holding the telephone. Ringing sound, unanswered. Puts the telephone down, as* McGONNIGAL's *face appears at the door.*

McGONNIGAL. Um, Stephen . . .

STEPHEN *looks at him blankly, then walks past him back into the corridor.*

McGONNIGAL. Could I just . . .

*And cut to the procession, from long shot, walking down the corridor. It stops again.*

STEPHEN. Where's Leary? (*Gazes at the throng,* LEARY *not amongst them.*)

AMANDA. Darling, don't *you* know?

STEPHEN (*smiles at her, a feeble smile*). Look, I'll join you later, I've just remembered.

*He goes off down one of the corridors, left. As he does so,* LEARY, *unseen by him, wanders back to the group, out of one of the offices, as* McGONNIGAL *suddenly hurries after* STEPHEN.
*Shot of* STEPHEN *walking down the corridor,* McGONNIGAL *hurrying after him, catching him in long shot. Then in on* McGONNIGAL's *face.*

McGONNIGAL (*as if with an effort*). I want to know why you haven't been passing on my notes to the actors? (STEPHEN *staring at him blankly.*) I must have made fifty notes, I've even tried to talk to Leary alone, but what with him nipping away all the time, and you getting between us, I haven't had a chance. In fact, (*working himself up*) I haven't had a chance since I arrived on the scene of my own play, which also doesn't have a chance, Stephen, and it doesn't have a chance because nobody, yourself included, and especially yourself, gives one goddamn about the style or the text, and now, with three hours before recording I can't get so much as a word with you. (*Stares boldly and slightly fearfully up at him.*)

STEPHEN. That's a very good point, Tim, don't you worry about it, leave it to me.

*His gaze is abstracted. He puts a comforting hand on* McGONNIGAL's *shoulder, and hurries off down the next corridor.*

**43. Interior.** *The front door step.* STEPHEN *going furtively through the front door, then running on his toes up the stairs, flings open the bedroom door. The bedroom is littered with clothes, bed unmade. He stands staring, then goes downstairs to the living-room, opens the door, goes in. Stares around, wanders* *across to the window, looks out.* GRIEG *is in the garden, doing up his belt. He raises his eyes, looks towards the window, sees* STEPHEN. *They stare at each other, then* STEPHEN *turns away, goes downstairs. Opens the kitchen door. Plates, cups, etc, everywhere. He comes out, is about to go on down the hall, then stops. Turns around. Looks at the basement door. Walks apprehensively towards it. Down into the basement, stops before* GRIEG's *door, then after a second, bends, looks through the key-hole. As seen through key-hole.* WENDY, *seen from in front, sitting on the bed, facing the door. She is tossled, dress partly opened, her legs spread carelessly. A mug of tea in her hand, her head bent over it. She raises her head, seems to be staring straight at him. Cut to:*

**44. Interior. Basement.** *Door, seen from* WENDY's *point of view. The door-knob turns, then slips back. Sound of feet running up the stairs, the front door slamming shut.* WENDY *continues to stare, then fiddles her hand across the bed, puts dark glasses on. Fade out. In on:*

**45. Interior. The Bedroom.** *Darkness. The door opens, in. A small light goes on, illuminating* WENDY's *face, sleeping. Sound of footsteps moving towards her. Her eyes open blearily, cut to* STEPHEN *standing over her, his briefcase in his hand, then cut back to* WENDY's *face, her mouth spreading in a semi-conscious, sexual grin, and cut to* STEPHEN's *face, as he turns away, and cut to:*

**46. Interior. The Living-room.** WENDY *sitting in an armchair, looking towards the window, and cut to* STEPHEN, *standing at the window, looking down. He turns suddenly, his face twisted with pain, then walks quickly out of the room.* WENDY *gets up, goes over to the window, raises it, looks out.*

**47. Exterior. Garden.** *Shot of* GRIEG, *from her point of view, bending over a patch of bush, small shears in his hand. He looks*

*up at her, looks down again. Puts the shears down. Then cut to*
STEPHEN, *walking quickly across the garden, approaches* GRIEG, *stands beside the shears. Cut back to* WENDY, *close-up, her lips open in excitement, then back to the garden from her point of view as* GRIEG, *still bending,* STEPHEN *bending beside him, picks up the shears.* STEPHEN *staring down at the back of* GRIEG's *neck as* GRIEG *still bending, holds out his hand. Cut back to* WENDY's *face, close-up, she closes her eyes in horror or in ecstacy, opens them, stares down.* GRIEG *is snipping away with the shears.* STEPHEN *is walking away. Sound of door slamming.*

**48. Interior.** STEPHEN's *footsteps. He comes into the room, brushes his hair away from his eyes, then goes across and sits down by the Hi-Fi set. Turns it on. Sits for a second,* WENDY *watching him from another chair. He sits facing ahead, then begins to nod, almost imperceptibly, his head to the music.* WENDY *adjusts her dark glasses. Fade out on this, and up on the two of them in the same position.* STEPHEN *staring at the television set,* WENDY *watching it indolently, the dark glasses pushed up to her forehead.*

*On the screen:* LEARY's *face, in his evening suit.* AMANDA *in profile.*

LEARY (*speaking in faked-up Coward voice*). My dear lady, we ought to have exchanged teething rings in the registry office, or perhaps one of those ebony do-dahs in the shape of our respective throats, because that's what we spend our time sinking our respective bridge-work into.

*As he concludes this,* STEPHEN *leans across, turns the set off. Sits staring ahead, then looks at* WENDY, *with her glasses up. She pokes them down with her finger, stares impassively back at him.* STEPHEN *gets up, walks across the room, to the door, goes out.* WENDY *watches. Gets up. The door opens again almost immediately,* STEPHEN *comes running across the room, his eyes and face mad, stands in front of* WENDY, *who remains sitting staring up at him. He begins to slap at her, crazy swattings. She makes a few weak defensive gestures, gets backed into a chair, her glasses knocked off.* STEPHEN *stands breathing heavily, making little crying noises.*

WENDY. Oh Stephen (*calmly and after a long pause*) he does *much* worse.

**49. Interior.** *Shot of bedroom, in disarray, clothes scattered everywhere. From below sounds of Bach, very low. Camera tracks around the room, takes in a heap of* WENDY's *knickers, then pans out, and down the stairs, and in on:*

**50. Interior. The Living-room.** *The Hi-Fi on.* WENDY *and* MR WYCHERLEY *over by the window.* STEPHEN *pouring a drink.* MRS WYCHERLEY *seated in one of the Barcelona chairs.*

MR WYCHERLEY. Still cultivating *your* garden, I see.

WENDY. Yes.

MR WYCHERLEY (*glances towards her. She remains staring down*). I take it he's settled down, then. (*Drily.*) For good. Eh, Stephen?

STEPHEN. I don't know. Do *you* think he has, darling?

WENDY (*smiles*). It looks like it.

*And cut to:*

MRS WYCHERLEY (*looking at* WENDY *and* MR WYCHERLEY, *their backs to her, still at the window, then looks at* STEPHEN, *who is now lolling in a chair, smoking a cheroot and playing with something out of sight*). I've been meaning to ask, what's the new play like, is it as stylish as the last?

STEPHEN. Not yet. But it will be. (*Slips the glasses on over his nose.*)

MRS WYCHERLEY (*again glances towards the window, where* MR WYCHERLEY *has just put his hand on* WENDY's arm). Just as long as you don't get yourself censored by that ghastly woman, the one that makes all the noise, you know what *my* feelings are about coloureds and illegits, but she talks as (*cutting to* MR WYCHERLEY, *his hand on* WENDY's *arm,* MRS WYCHERLEY's *voice over*) if the whole country was an absolute marsh of vice and licence and what have you . . . (*cut back to* MRS WYCHERLEY, *staring towards*

MR WYCHERLEY) which I must say I take great personal exception to, *and* I like the right (*turning to* STEPHEN) not to look at what's there to be seen, after all if people don't like it they can always switch off, can't they?

*And cut back to:*

MR WYCHERLEY (*smiles at* WENDY, *who turns towards him. His hand still on her shoulder*). All right then?

WENDY (*vaguely*). Fine thanks. (*Moves away from him, he lets his arm drop.*)

*Cut to* STEPHEN, *who is watching* MR WYCHERLEY *with a little smile,* MR WYCHERLEY *looks towards him, meets his eyes,* STEPHEN's *smile remains, small but triumphant.* MR WYCHERLEY *turns back to the window, and* WENDY *crosses to* STEPHEN, *as:*

MRS WYCHERLEY. Which I must say, I quite frequently find myself having to do. Switch off, I mean.

STEPHEN *smiling at* WENDY. WENDY *smiling back at him, nicely and yet almost impersonally, and from her to* MR WYCHERLEY, *turning away to stare coldly out of the window down on the garden, and finally to:*


**51. Exterior. Garden.** GRIEG *standing in the centre of the garden, his hands on his hips, staring up, seen from* MR WYCHERLEY's *point of view, and seeming to make, to the rising sound of Bach, a slow, obscene gesture, and:*

**ENDS**